Long Narrative
(Nineteenth Century)

SECOND SERIES

Edited by
George G. Loane, M.A.

MACMILLAN AND CO., LIMITED
ST. MARTIN'S STREET, LONDON
1927

COPYRIGHT

PRINTED IN GREAT BRITAIN

CONTENTS

		PAGE
INTRODUCTION		vii
I. MICHAEL	Wordsworth	1
II. MAZEPPA'S RIDE	Byron	17
III. LAMIA	Keats	35
IV. THE HOLY GRAIL	Tennyson	59
V. THE WRITING ON THE IMAGE	Morris	90
VI. THE SICK KING IN BOKHARA	Arnold	102
VII. MULÉYKEH	Browning	111
NOTES		119
QUESTIONS AND SUBJECTS FOR ESSAYS		122
HELPS TO FURTHER STUDY		128

INTRODUCTION

I. MICHAEL

WE have here Wordsworth at his best and most characteristic: the simple and expressive language rising at times to poignant eloquence; the rustic scene; the pathos 'trenchant but not tender—an iron pathos'; and above all the deep and sympathetic knowledge of the human heart. In a letter to Charles Fox, Wordsworth speaks of *Michael* and *The Brothers* as poems written with a view to show 'that men who do not wear fine clothes can feel deeply'; and it is largely owing to him that the sentiment now strikes us as a truism. The personages and the sheepfold are drawn from the life, being near the poet's home at Grasmere.

II. MAZEPPA'S RIDE

Resting at night during the retreat from Pultowa, the aged Cossack prince (or hetman) Mazeppa relates to Charles XII. how he expiated a sin of early youth. A few dry sentences in Voltaire's *History* gave Byron's imagination material for a spirited and impressive poem. The wolves and the wild horses are finely described, and the sufferings of Mazeppa are made vivid without being disgusting. The swift gallop of the verse slows down suitably in the reflective passages, which, so far from impeding the narrative, help us to realize the lapse of time. The poem well illustrates Byron's 'wonderful power of vividly conceiving a single incident, and making us see and feel it too.'

III. LAMIA

In the moving and dignified preface to *Endymion*, Keats had expressed some hope that while it was dwindling he might be plotting, and fitting himself for verses fit to live. That hope was fulfilled in the famous volume of 1820, containing *Lamia, The Eve of St. Agnes, Isabella, Hyperion* and the great Odes. Both in versification and in narrative power *Lamia* is a great advance on the earlier work, and owes much to his study of Dryden's *Fables*. Except for a few lines which maturer judgement would surely have altered, it is with its 'melodious, lovely and surprising phrases' a beautiful poem, even if not quite so beautiful as *The Eve of St. Agnes*. Lamia in his hands is no vulgar witch but a strange and spiritually accomplished person with whom it may be possible to sympathize. Of all his additions to the prose original, the greatest is the addition of pity and love.

IV. THE HOLY GRAIL

Ten years after the publication of the first four *Idylls of the King*—Enid, Vivien, Elaine, Guinevere—Tennyson grappled with the subject of the Grail, which had been in his mind from the first. He wrote it rapidly, condensing with great skill the many and discordant legends of antiquity. His son recalled the *inspired* way he chanted the different parts of the poem as they were composed. He made it the vehicle of some of his own deepest thoughts: 'One of the most imaginative of my poems,' he calls it; 'I have expressed there my strong feeling as to the Reality of the Unseen.'

INTRODUCTION

And he quoted three lines near the end as being the (spiritually) central lines of the *Idylls*:

> 'In moments when he feels he cannot die,
> And knows himself no vision to himself,
> Nor the High God a vision.'

The rich stores of thought, phrase and picture contrast with the pathetic simplicity of Sir Thomas Malory.

V. THE WRITING ON THE IMAGE

This poem is one of the twenty-four tales included in *The Earthly Paradise*. It is shorter and less varied than most of its companions, and gives no opportunity for those intimate descriptions of scenery in which Morris revelled. But it is told with unusual and masterly conciseness, and the rather tired view of life is characteristic. The great personal energy of Morris is oddly wanting in his writing. Atmospheric charm, large effects, a low-pitched flight, ease and level excellence are qualities which have been rightly ascribed to him. 'There is not a great line, there are but few separably fine lines, in the whole of his work. But every line has distinction, and every line is in its place.' This is just and high praise.

VI. THE SICK KING IN BOKHARA

It is worth considering how a poem so quiet and unadorned can set so vividly before us 'the hot suffering eastern life.' It is a typical example of the classic restraint, the hatred of sensationalism characteristic of Arnold. Here are none even of the elaborate Homeric similes introduced into *Sohrab and Rustum*, no ingenious phrases or striking epithets, hardly any scenery, very little action: yet the effect is memorable, 'these things come in and remain with us.' The colour is no doubt heightened by the few eastern names introduced, but they do not spoil the simplicity of the narrative, or impair the evident sincerity of the writer. Arnold has not the glowing imagination which could carry the audacities of a poet like Keats; but within his limits his touch is sure, and in the halls of poesy there are many mansions.

VII. MULÉYKEH

Little need be added to Edward Dowden's memorable words on 'one of the most delightful of Browning's later poems, uniting as it does the poetry of the rapture of swift motion with the poetry of high-hearted passion. The narrative leads up to a supreme moment, and this resolves itself through a paradox of the heart. . . . Browning's casuistry is not argumentative; it lies in an appeal to some passion or some intuition that is above our common levels of passion or of insight, and his power of uplifting his reader for even a moment into this higher mood is his special gift as a poet. We can return safely enough to the common ground, but we return with a possession which instructs the heart.' Mr. Arthur Symons notes that the tale 'is told in singularly fine verse, and in a remarkably clear, simple, yet elevated style.'

WILLIAM WORDSWORTH

MICHAEL

A PASTORAL POEM

IF from the public way you turn your steps
Up the tumultuous brook of Greenhead Ghyll,
You will suppose that with an upright path
Your feet must struggle ; in such bold ascent
The pastoral mountains front you, face to face.
But, courage ! for around that boisterous brook
The mountains have all opened out themselves,
And made a hidden valley of their own.
No habitation can be seen ; but they
Who journey thither find themselves alone   10
With a few sheep, with rocks and stones, and kites
That overhead are sailing in the sky.
It is in truth an utter solitude ;
Nor should I have made mention of this Dell
But for one object which you might pass by,
Might see and notice not.   Beside the brook
Appears a straggling heap of unhewn stones !
And to that simple object appertains
A story—unenriched with strange events,
Yet not unfit, I deem, for the fireside,   20
Or for the summer shade.   It was the first
Of those domestic tales that spake to me

Of shepherds, dwellers in the valleys, men
Whom I already loved ;—not verily
For their own sakes, but for the fields and hills
Where was their occupation and abode.
And hence this Tale, while I was yet a Boy
Careless of books, yet having felt the power
Of Nature, by the gentle agency
Of natural objects, led me on to feel 30
For passions that were not my own, and think
(At random and imperfectly indeed)
On man, the heart of man, and human life.
Therefore, although it be a history
Homely and rude, I will relate the same
For the delight of a few natural hearts ;
And, with yet fonder feeling, for the sake
Of youthful Poets, who among these hills
Will be my second self when I am gone.

 Upon the forest-side in Grasmere Vale 40
There dwelt a Shepherd, Michael was his name ;
An old man, stout of heart, and strong of limb.
His bodily frame had been from youth to age
Of an unusual strength : his mind was keen,
Intense, and frugal, apt for all affairs,
And in his shepherd's calling he was prompt
And watchful more than ordinary men.
Hence had he learned the meaning of all winds,
Of blasts of every tone ; and, oftentimes,
When others heeded not, He heard the South 50
Make subterraneous music, like the noise
Of bagpipers on distant Highland hills.
The Shepherd, at such warning, of his flock
Bethought him, and he to himself would say,

"The winds are now devising work for me!"
And, truly, at all times, the storm, that drives
The traveller to a shelter, summoned him
Up to the mountains : he had been alone
Amid the heart of many thousand mists,
That came to him, and left him, on the heights. 60
So lived he till his eightieth year was past.
And grossly that man errs, who should suppose
That the green valleys, and the streams and rocks,
Were things indifferent to the Shepherd's thoughts.
Fields, where with cheerful spirits he had breathed
The common air ; hills, which with vigorous step
He had so often climbed ; which had impressed
So many incidents upon his mind
Of hardship, skill or courage, joy or fear ;
Which, like a book, preserved the memory 70
Of the dumb animals, whom he had saved,
Had fed or sheltered, linking to such acts
The certainty of honourable gain ;
Those fields, those hills—what could they less ? had laid
Strong hold on his affections, were to him
A pleasurable feeling of blind love,
The pleasure which there is in life itself.

   His days had not been passed in singleness.
His Helpmate was a comely matron, old—
Though younger than himself full twenty years. 80
She was a woman of a stirring life,
Whose heart was in her house : two wheels she had
Of antique form ; this large, for spinning wool ;
That small, for flax ; and if one wheel had rest
It was because the other was at work.
The Pair had but one inmate in their house,

An only Child, who had been born to them
When Michael, telling o'er his years, began
To deem that he was old,—in shepherd's phrase,
With one foot in the grave. This only Son,   90
With two brave sheep-dogs tried in many a storm,
The one of an inestimable worth,
Made all their household. I may truly say,
That they were as a proverb in the vale
For endless industry. When day was gone,
And from their occupations out of doors
The Son and Father were come home, even then,
Their labour did not cease ; unless when all
Turned to the cleanly supper-board, and there,
Each with a mess of pottage and skimmed milk,   100
Sat round the basket piled with oaten cakes,
And their plain home-made cheese. Yet when the meal
Was ended, Luke (for so the Son was named)
And his old Father both betook themselves
To such convenient work as might employ
Their hands by the fireside ; perhaps to card
Wool for the Housewife's spindle, or repair
Some injury done to sickle, flail, or scythe,
Or other implement of house or field.

    Down from the ceiling, by the chimney's edge,   110
That in our ancient uncouth country style
With huge and black projection overbrowed
Large space beneath, as duly as the light
Of day grew dim the Housewife hung a lamp ;
An aged utensil, which had performed
Service beyond all others of its kind.
Early at evening did it burn—and late,
Surviving comrade of uncounted hours,

Which, going by from year to year, had found,
And left, the couple neither gay perhaps   120
Nor cheerful, yet with objects and with hopes,
Living a life of eager industry.
And now, when Luke had reached his eighteenth year,
There by the light of this old lamp they sate,
Father and Son, while far into the night
The Housewife plied her own peculiar work,
Making the cottage through the silent hours
Murmur as with the sound of summer flies.
This light was famous in its neighbourhood,
And was a public symbol of the life   130
That thrifty Pair had lived. For, as it chanced,
Their cottage on a plot of rising ground
Stood single, with large prospect, north and south,
High into Easedale, up to Dunmail-Raise,
And westward to the village near the lake ;
And from this constant light, so regular
And so far seen, the House itself, by all
Who dwelt within the limits of the vale,
Both old and young, was named THE EVENING STAR.

    Thus living on through such a length of years,   140
The Shepherd, if he loved himself, must needs
Have loved his Helpmate ; but to Michael's heart
This son of his old age was yet more dear—
Less from instinctive tenderness, the same
Fond spirit that blindly works in the blood of all—
Than that a child, more than all other gifts
That earth can offer to declining man,
Brings hope with it, and forward-looking thoughts,
And stirrings of inquietude, when they
By tendency of nature needs must fail.   150

Exceeding was the love he bare to him,
His heart and his heart's joy! For oftentimes
Old Michael, while he was a babe in arms,
Had done him female service, not alone
For pastime and delight, as is the use
Of fathers, but with patient mind enforced
To acts of tenderness; and he had rocked
His cradle, as with a woman's gentle hand.

And, in a later time, ere yet the Boy
Had put on boy's attire, did Michael love,   160
Albeit of a stern unbending mind,
To have the Young-one in his sight, when he
Wrought in the field, or on his shepherd's stool
Sate with a fettered sheep before him stretched
Under the large old oak, that near his door
Stood single, and, from matchless depth of shade,
Chosen for the Shearer's covert from the sun,
Thence in our rustic dialect was called
The CLIPPING TREE, a name which yet it bears.
There, while they two were sitting in the shade,   170
With others round them, earnest all and blithe,
Would Michael exercise his heart with looks
Of fond correction and reproof bestowed
Upon the Child, if he disturbed the sheep
By catching at their legs, or with his shouts
Scared them, while they lay still beneath the shears.

And when by Heaven's good grace the boy grew up
A healthy Lad, and carried in his cheek
Two steady roses that were five years old;
Then Michael from a winter coppice cut   180
With his own hand a sapling, which he hooped
With iron, making it throughout in all

Due requisites a perfect shepherd's staff,
And gave it to the Boy ; wherewith equipt
He as a watchman oftentimes was placed
At gate or gap, to stem or turn the flock ;
And, to his office prematurely called,
There stood the urchin, as you will divine,
Something between a hindrance and a help ;
And for this cause not always, I believe, 190
Receiving from his Father hire of praise ;
Though nought was left undone which staff, or voice,
Or looks, or threatening gestures, could perform.

 But soon as Luke, full ten years old, could stand
Against the mountain blasts ; and to the heights,
Not fearing toil, nor length of weary ways,
He with his Father daily went, and they
Were as companions, why should I relate
That objects which the Shepherd loved before
Were dearer now ? that from the Boy there came 200
Feelings and emanations—things which were
Light to the sun and music to the wind ;
And that the old Man's heart seemed born again ?

 Thus in his father's sight the Boy grew up :
And now, when he had reached his eighteenth year,
He was his comfort and his daily hope.

 While in this sort the simple household lived
From day to day, to Michael's ear there came
Distressful tidings. Long before the time
Of which I speak, the Shepherd had been bound 210
In surety for his brother's son, a man
Of an industrious life, and ample means ;
But unforeseen misfortunes suddenly
Had prest upon him ; and old Michael now

Was summoned to discharge the forfeiture,
A grievous penalty, but little less
Than half his substance. This unlooked-for claim,
At the first hearing, for a moment took
More hope out of his life than he supposed
That any old man ever could have lost. 220
As soon as he had armed himself with strength
To look his trouble in the face, it seemed
The Shepherd's sole resource to sell at once
A portion of his patrimonial fields.
Such was his first resolve ; he thought again,
And his heart failed him. " Isabel," said he,
Two evenings after he had heard the news,
" I have been toiling more than seventy years,
And in the open sunshine of God's love
Have we all lived ; yet if these fields of ours 230
Should pass into a stranger's hand, I think
That I could not lie quiet in my grave.
Our lot is a hard lot ; the sun himself
Has scarcely been more diligent than I ;
And I have lived to be a fool at last
To my own family. An evil man
That was, and made an evil choice, if he
Were false to us ; and if he were not false,
There are ten thousand to whom loss like this
Had been no sorrow. I forgive him ;—but 240
'Twere better to be dumb than to talk thus.

 When I began, my purpose was to speak
Of remedies and of a cheerful hope.
Our Luke shall leave us, Isabel ; the land
Shall not go from us, and it shall be free ;
He shall possess it, free as is the wind

That passes over it. We have, thou knows't,
Another kinsman—he will be our friend
In this distress. He is a prosperous man,
Thriving in trade—and Luke to him shall go,   250
And with his kinsman's help and his own thrift
He quickly will repair this loss, and then
He may return to us. If here he stay,
What can be done ? Where every one is poor,
What can be gained ? "
                      At this the old Man paused,
And Isabel sat silent, for her mind
Was busy, looking back into past times.
There's Richard Bateman, thought she to herself,
He was a parish-boy—at the church-door
They made a gathering for him, shillings, pence   260
And halfpennies, wherewith the neighbours bought
A basket, which they filled with ped'ar's wares ;
And, with this basket on his arm, the lad
Went up to London, found a master there,
Who, out of many, chose the trusty boy
To go and overlook his merchandise
Beyond the seas ; where he grew wondrous rich,
And left estates and monies to the poor,
And, at his birth-place, built a chapel, floored
With marble which he sent from foreign lands.   270
These thoughts, and many others of like sort,
Passed quickly through the mind of Isabel,
And her face brightened. The old Man was glad,
And thus resumed :—" Well, Isabel ! this scheme
These two days, has been meat and drink to me.
Far more than we have lost is left us yet.
—We have enough—I wish indeed that I

Were younger ;—but this hope is a good hope.
—Make ready Luke's best garments, of the best
Buy for him more, and let us send him forth 280
To-morrow, or the next day, or to-night :
—If he *could* go, the Boy should go to-night."
Here Michael ceased, and to the fields went forth
With a light heart. The Housewife for five days
Was restless morn and night, and all day long
Wrought on with her best fingers to prepare
Things needful for the journey of her son.
But Isabel was glad when Sunday came
To stop her in her work : for, when she lay
By Michael's side, she through the last two nights 290
Heard him, how he was troubled in his sleep :
And when they rose at morning she could see
That all his hopes were gone. That day at noon
She said to Luke, while they two by themselves
Were sitting at the door, " Thou must not go :
We have no other Child but thee to lose,
None to remember—do not go away,
For if thou leave thy Father he will die."
The Youth made answer with a jocund voice ;
And Isabel, when she had told her fears, 300
Recovered heart. That evening her best fare
Did she bring forth, and all together sat
Like happy people round a Christmas fire.

With daylight Isabel resumed her work ;
And all the ensuing week the house appeared
As cheerful as a grove in Spring : at length
The expected letter from their kinsman came,
With kind assurances that he would do
His utmost for the welfare of the Boy ;

To which, requests were added, that forthwith
He might be sent to him. Ten times or more
The letter was read over ; Isabel
Went forth to show it to the neighbours round ;
Nor was there at that time on English land
A prouder heart than Luke's. When Isabel
Had to her house returned, the old Man said,
" He shall depart to-morrow." To this word
The Housewife answered, talking much of things
Which, if at such short notice he should go,
Would surely be forgotten. But at length
She gave consent, and Michael was at ease.
   Near the tumultuous brook of Greenhead Ghyll,
In that deep valley, Michael had designed
To build a Sheepfold ; and, before he heard
The tidings of his melancholy loss,
For this same purpose he had gathered up
A heap of stones, which by the streamlet's edge
Lay thrown together, ready for the work.
With Luke that evening thitherward he walked :
And soon as they had reached the place he stopped,
And thus the old Man spake to him :—" My Son,
To-morrow thou wilt leave me : with full heart
I look upon thee, for thou art the same
That wert a promise to me ere thy birth,
And all thy life hast been my daily joy.
I will relate to thee some little part
Of our two histories ; 'twill do thee good
When thou art from me, even if I should touch
On things thou canst not know of.—After thou
First cam'st into the world—as oft befalls
To new-born infants—thou didst sleep away

Two days, and blessings from thy Father's tongue
Then fell upon thee. Day by day passed on,
And still I loved thee with increasing love.
Never to living ear came sweeter sounds
Than when I heard thee by our own fireside
First uttering, without words, a natural tune;
While thou, a feeding babe, didst in thy joy
Sing at thy Mother's breast. Month followed month,
And in the open fields my life was passed   350
And on the mountains; else I think that thou
Hadst been brought up upon thy Father's knees.
But we were playmates, Luke: among these hills,
As well thou knowest, in us the old and young
Have played together, nor with me didst thou
Lack any pleasure which a boy can know."
Luke had a manly heart; but at these words
He sobbed aloud. The old Man grasped his hand,
And said, " Nay, do not take it so—I see
That these are things of which I need not speak.   360
—Even to the utmost I have been to thee
A kind and a good Father: and herein
I but repay a gift which I myself
Received at others' hands; for, though now old
Beyond the common life of man, I still
Remember them who loved me in my youth.
Both of them sleep together: here they lived,
As all their Forefathers had done; and when
At length their time was come, they were not loth
To give their bodies to the family mould.   370
I wished that thou should'st live the life they lived:
But, 'tis a long time to look back, my Son,
And see so little gain from threescore years.

MICHAEL

These fields were burthened when they came to me ;
Till I was forty years of age, not more
Than half of my inheritance was mine.
I toiled and toiled ; God blessed me in my work,
And till these three weeks past the land was free.
—It looks as if it never could endure
Another Master. Heaven forgive me, Luke,   380
If I judge ill for thee, but it seems good
That thou should'st go."
                       At this the old Man paused ;
Then, pointing to the stones near which they stood,
Thus, after a short silence, he resumed :
" This was a work for us ; and now, my Son,
It is a work for me. But, lay one stone—
Here, lay it for me, Luke, with thine own hands.
Nay, Boy, be of good hope ;—we both may live
To see a better day. At eighty-four
I still am strong and hale ;—do thou thy part ;   390
I will do mine.—I will begin again
With many tasks that were resigned to thee :
Up to the heights, and in among the storms,
Will I without thee go again, and do
All works which I was wont to do alone,
Before I knew thy face.—Heaven bless thee, Boy !
Thy heart these two weeks has been beating fast
With many hopes ; it should be so—yes—yes—
I knew that thou could'st never have a wish
To leave me, Luke : thou hast been bound to me   400
Only by links of love : when thou art gone,
What will be left to us !—But, I forget
My purposes. Lay now the corner-stone,
As I requested ; and hereafter, Luke,

When thou art gone away, should evil men
Be thy companions, think of me, my Son,
And of this moment; hither turn thy thoughts,
And God will strengthen thee: amid all fear
And all temptation, Luke, I pray that thou
May'st bear in mind the life thy Fathers lived,   410
Who, being innocent, did for that cause
Bestir them in good deeds. Now, fare thee well—
When thou return'st, thou in this place wilt see
A work which is not here: a covenant
'Twill be between us; but, whatever fate
Befall thee, I shall love thee to the last,
And bear thy memory with me to the grave."
   The Shepherd ended here; and Luke stooped down,
And, as his Father had requested, laid
The first stone of the Sheepfold. At the sight   420
The old Man's grief broke from him; to his heart
He pressed his Son, he kissèd him and wept;
And to the house together they returned.
—Hushed was that House in peace, or seeming peace,
Ere the night fell:—with morrow's dawn the Boy
Began his journey, and when he had reached
The public way, he put on a bold face;
And all the neighbours, as he passed their doors,
Came forth with wishes and with farewell prayers,
That followed him till he was out of sight.   430
   A good report did from their Kinsman come,
Of Luke and his well-doing: and the Boy
Wrote loving letters, full of wondrous news,
Which, as the Housewife phrased it, were throughout
"The prettiest letters that were ever seen."
Both parents read them with rejoicing hearts.

So, many months passed on : and once again
The Shepherd went about his daily work
With confident and cheerful thoughts ; and now
Sometimes when he could find a leisure hour   440
He to that valley took his way, and there
Wrought at the Sheepfold. Meantime Luke began
To slacken in his duty ; and, at length,
He in the dissolute city gave himself
To evil courses : ignominy and shame
Fell on him, so that he was driven at last
To seek a hiding-place beyond the seas.
  There is a comfort in the strength of love ;
'Twill make a thing endurable, which else
Would overset the brain, or break the heart :   450
I have conversed with more than one who well
Remember the old Man, and what he was
Years after he had heard this heavy news.
His bodily frame had been from youth to age
Of an unusual strength. Among the rocks
He went, and still looked up to sun and cloud,
And listened to the wind ; and, as before,
Performed all kinds of labour for his sheep,
And for the land, his small inheritance.
And to that hollow dell from time to time   460
Did he repair, to build the Fold of which
His flock had need. 'Tis not forgotten yet
The pity which was then in every heart
For the old Man—and 'tis believed by all
That many and many a day he thither went,
And never lifted up a single stone.
  There, by the Sheepfold, sometimes was he seen
Sitting alone, or with his faithful Dog,

Then old, beside him, lying at his feet.
The length of full seven years, from time to time,   470
He at the building of this Sheepfold wrought,
And left the work unfinished when he died.
Three years, or little more, did Isabel
Survive her Husband : at her death the estate
Was sold, and went into a stranger's hand.
The Cottage which was named the EVENING STAR
Is gone—the ploughshare has been through the ground
On which it stood ; great changes have been wrought
In all the neighbourhood :—yet the oak is left
That grew beside their door ; and the remains   480
Of the unfinished Sheepfold may be seen
Beside the boisterous brook of Greenhead Ghyll.

GEORGE GORDON, LORD BYRON

MAZEPPA'S RIDE

I

" ' BRING forth the horse ! '—the horse was brought ;
  In truth, he was a noble steed,
  A Tartar of the Ukraine breed,
Who look'd as though the speed of thought
Were in his limbs ; but he was wild,
  Wild as the wild deer, and untaught,
With spur and bridle undefiled—
  'Twas but a day he had been caught ;
And snorting, with erected mane,
And struggling fiercely, but in vain,   10
In the full foam of wrath and dread
To me the desert-born was led :
They bound me on, that menial throng,
Upon his back with many a thong ;
Then loosed him with a sudden lash—
Away !—away !—and on we dash !
Torrents less rapid and less rash.

II

" Away !—away ! My breath was gone—
I saw not where he hurried on :
'Twas scarcely yet the break of day,   20
And on he foam'd—away !—away !

The last of human sounds which rose,
As I was darted from my foes,
Was the wild shout of savage laughter,
Which on the wind came roaring after
A moment from that rabble rout:
With sudden wrath I wrench'd my head,
    And snapp'd the cord, which to the mane
    Had bound my neck in lieu of rein,
And, writhing half my form about,
Howl'd back my curse; but 'midst the tread,
The thunder of my courser's speed,
Perchance they did not hear nor heed: 30
It vexes me—for I would fain
Have paid their insult back again.
I paid it well in after days:
There is not of that castle gate,
Its drawbridge and portcullis' weight,
Stone, bar, moat, bridge, or barrier left;
Nor of its fields a blade of grass,   40
    Save what grows on a ridge of wall,
    Where stood the hearth-stone of the hall;
And many a time ye there might pass,
Nor dream that e'er that fortress was;
I saw its turrets in a blaze,
Their crackling battlements all cleft,
    And the hot lead pour down like rain
From off the scorch'd and blackening roof,
Whose thickness was not vengeance-proof.
    They little thought that day of pain,   50
When launched, as on the lightning's flash,
They bade me to destruction dash,
    That one day I should come again,

With twice five thousand horse, to thank—
  The Count for his uncourteous ride.
They play'd me then a bitter prank,
  When, with the wild horse for my guide,
They bound me to his foaming flank :
At length I play'd them one as frank—
For time at last sets all things even—   60
  And if we do but watch the hour,
There never yet was human power
Which could evade, if unforgiven,
The patient search and vigil long
Of him who treasures up a wrong.

III

" Away, away, my steed and I,
  Upon the pinions of the wind,
  All human dwellings left behind ·
We sped like meteors through the sky,
When with its crackling sound the night   70
Is chequer'd with the northern light :
Town—village—none were on our track,
  But a wild plain of far extent,
And bounded by a forest black ;
  And, save the scarce seen battlement
On distant heights of some strong hold,
Against the Tartars built of old,
No trace of man. The year before
A Turkish army had marched o'er ;
And where the Spahi's hoof hath trod,   80
The verdure flies the bloody sod :
The sky was dull, and dim, and gray,
  And a low breeze crept moaning by—

I could have answer'd with a sigh—
But fast we fled, away, away,
And I could neither sigh nor pray;
And my cold sweat-drops fell like rain
Upon the courser's bristling mane;
But, snorting still with rage and fear,
He flew upon his far career: 90
At times I almost thought, indeed,
He must have slacken'd in his speed;
But no—my bound and slender frame
  Was nothing to his angry might,
And merely like a spur became :
Each motion which I made to free
My swoln limbs from their agony
  Increased his fury and affright :
I tried my voice,—'twas faint and low,
But yet he swerved as from a blow;   100
And, starting to each accent, sprang
As from a sudden trumpet's clang :
Meantime my cords were wet with gore,
Which, oozing through my limbs, ran o'er;
And in my tongue the thirst became
A something fierier far than flame.

IV

"We near'd the wild wood—'twas so wide,
I saw no bounds on either side ;
'Twas studded with old sturdy trees,
That bent not to the roughest breeze   110
Which howls down from Siberia's waste,
And strips the forest in its haste,—
But these were few and far between,

Set thick with shrubs more young and green,
Luxuriant with their annual leaves,
Ere strown by those autumnal eves
That nip the forest's foliage dead,
Discolour'd with a lifeless red,
Which stands thereon like stiffen'd gore
Upon the slain when battle's o'er, 120
And some long winter's night hath shed
Its frost o'er every tombless head,
So cold and stark the raven's beak
May peck unpierced each frozen cheek:
'Twas a wild waste of underwood,
And here and there a chestnut stood,
The strong oak, and the hardy pine;
　But far apart—and well it were,
Or else a different lot were mine—
　The boughs gave way, and did not tear 130
My limbs; and I found strength to bear
My wounds, already scarr'd with cold;
My bonds forbade to loose my hold.
We rustled through the leaves like wind,
Left shrubs, and trees, and wolves behind;
By night I heard them on the track,
Their troop came hard upon our back,
With their long gallop, which can tire
The hound's deep hate, and hunter's fire:
Where'er we flew they followed on, 140
Nor left us with the morning sun;
Behind I saw them, scarce a rood,
At day-break winding through the wood,
And through the night had heard their feet
Their stealing, rustling step repeat.

Oh! how I wish'd for spear or sword,
At least to die amidst the horde,
And perish—if it must be so—
At bay, destroying many a foe!
When first my courser's race begun, 150
I wish'd the goal already won;
But now I doubted strength and speed.
Vain doubt! his swift and savage breed
Had nerved him like the mountain-roe;
Nor faster falls the blinding snow
Which whelms the peasant near the door
Whose threshold he shall cross no more,
Bewilder'd with the dazzling blast,
Than through the forest-paths he pass'd—
Untired, untamed, and worse than wild; 160
All furious as a favour'd child
Balk'd of its wish; or fiercer still—
A woman piqued—who has her will.

V

" The wood was past; 'twas more than noon,
But chill the air, although in June;
Or it might be my veins ran cold—
Prolong'd endurance tames the bold:
And I was then not what I seem,
But headlong as a wintry stream,
And wore my feelings out before 170
I well could count their causes o'er:
And what with fury, fear, and wrath,
The tortures which beset my path,
Cold, hunger, sorrow, shame, distress,
Thus bound in nature's nakedness;

Sprung from a race whose rising blood,
When stirr'd beyond its calmer mood,
And trodden hard upon, is like
The rattle-snake's, in act to strike,
What marvel if this worn-out trunk   180
Beneath its woes a moment sunk?
The earth gave way, the skies roll'd round,
I seem'd to sink upon the ground;
But err'd, for I was fastly bound.
My heart turn'd sick, my brain grew sore,
And throbb'd awhile, then beat no more:
The skies spun like a mighty wheel;
I saw the trees like drunkards reel,
And a slight flash sprang o'er my eyes,
Which saw no farther: he who dies   190
Can die no more than then I died.
O'ertortured by that ghastly ride,
I felt the blackness come and go,
   And strove to wake; but could not make
My senses climb up from below:
I felt as on a plank at sea,
When all the waves that dash o'er thee,
At the same time upheave and whelm,
And hurl thee towards a desert realm.
My undulating life was as   200
The fancied lights that flitting pass
Our shut eyes in deep midnight, when
Fever begins upon the brain;
But soon it pass'd, with little pain,
   But a confusion worse than such:
   I own that I should deem it much,
Dying, to feel the same again;

And yet I do suppose we must
Feel far more ere we turn to dust:
No matter; I have bared my brow   210
Full in Death's face—before—and now.

VI

" My thoughts came back; where was I?   Cold,
    And numb, and giddy: pulse by pulse
Life reassumed its lingering hold,
And throb by throb; till grown a pang
    Which for a moment would convulse,
    My blood reflow'd, though thick and chill;
My ear with uncouth noises rang,
    My heart began once more to thrill;
My sight return'd, though dim; alas!   220
And thicken'd, as it were, with glass.
Methought the dash of waves was nigh;
There was a gleam too of the sky,
Studded with stars;—it is no dream;
The wild horse swims the wilder stream!
The bright broad river's gushing tide
Sweeps, winding onward, far and wide,
And we are half-way, struggling o'er
To yon unknown and silent shore.
The waters broke my hollow trance,   230
And with a temporary strength
    My stiffen'd limbs were rebaptized.
My courser's broad breast proudly braves,
And dashes off the ascending waves,
And onward we advance!
We reach the slippery shore at length,
    A haven I but little prized,

For all behind was dark and drear,
And all before was night and fear.
How many hours of night or day
In those suspended pangs I lay,
I could not tell ; I scarcely knew
If this were human breath I drew.

VII

" With glossy skin, and dripping mane,
   And reeling limbs, and reeking flank,
The wild steed's sinewy nerves still strain
   Up the repelling bank.
We gain the top : a boundless plain
Spreads through the shadow of the night,
   And onward, onward, onward, seems,
   Like precipices in our dreams,
To stretch beyond the sight ;
And here and there a speck of white,
   Or scatter'd spot of dusky green,
In masses broke into the light,
As rose the moon upon my right :
   But nought distinctly seen
In the dim waste would indicate
The omen of a cottage gate ;
No twinkling taper from afar
Stood like a hospitable star ;
Not even an ignis-fatuus rose
To make him merry with my woes :
   That very cheat had cheer'd me then !
Although detected, welcome still,
Reminding me, through every ill,
   Of the abodes of men.

VIII

"Onward we went—but slack and slow;
His savage force at length o'erspent,
The drooping courser, faint and low, 270
All feebly foaming went.
A sickly infant had had power
To guide him forward in that hour:
But useless all to me:
His new-born tameness nought avail'd—
My limbs were bound; my force had fail'd,
Perchance, had they been free.
With feeble effort still I tried
To rend the bonds so starkly tied—
But still it was in vain; 280
My limbs were only wrung the more,
And soon the idle strife gave o'er,
Which but prolong'd their pain:
The dizzy race seem'd almost done,
Although no goal was nearly won:
Some streaks announced the coming sun—
How slow, alas! he came!
Methought that mist of dawning gray
Would never dapple into day;
How heavily it roll'd away— 290
Before the eastern flame
Rose crimson, and deposed the stars,
And call'd the radiance from their cars,
And fill'd the earth, from his deep throne,
With lonely lustre, all his own.

IX

"Up rose the sun; the mists were curl'd
Back from the solitary world
Which lay around, behind, before.
What booted it to traverse o'er
Plain, forest, river? Man nor brute,   300
Nor dint of hoof, nor print of foot,
Lay in the wild luxuriant soil;
No sign of travel, none of toil;
The very air was mute;
And not an insect's shrill small horn,
Nor matin bird's new voice was borne
From herb nor thicket. Many a werst,
Panting as if his heart would burst,
The weary brute still stagger'd on;
And still we were—or seem'd—alone.   310
At length, while reeling on our way,
Methought I heard a courser neigh,
From out yon tuft of blackening firs.
Is it the wind those branches stirs?
No, no! from out the forest prance
  A trampling troop; I see them come!
In one vast squadron they advance!
  I strove to cry—my lips were dumb.
The steeds rush on in plunging pride;
But where are they the reins to guide?   320
A thousand horse, and none to ride!
With flowing tail, and flying mane,
Wide nostrils never stretch'd by pain,
Mouths bloodless to the bit or rein,

And feet that iron never shod,
And flanks unscarr'd by spur or rod,
A thousand horse, the wild, the free,
Like waves that follow o'er the sea,
   Came thickly thundering on,
As if our faint approach to meet;   330
The sight re-nerved my courser's feet,
A moment staggering, feebly fleet,
A moment, with a faint low neigh,
   He answered, and then fell;
With gasps and glazing eyes he lay,
   And reeking limbs immoveable,
      His first and last career is done!
On came the troop—they saw him stoop,
   They saw me strangely bound along
   His back with many a bloody thong: 340
They stop—they start—they snuff the air,
Gallop a moment here and there,
Approach, retire, wheel round and round,
Then plunging back with sudden bound,
Headed by one black mighty steed,
Who seem'd the patriarch of his breed,
   Without a single speck or hair
Of white upon his shaggy hide;
They snort—they foam—neigh—swerve aside,
And backward to the forest fly,   350
By instinct, from a human eye.—
   They left me there to my despair,
Link'd to the dead and stiffening wretch,
Whose lifeless limbs beneath me stretch,
Relieved from that unwonted weight,
From whence I could not extricate

Nor him nor me—and there we lay,
  The dying on the dead!
I little deem'd another day
  Would see my houseless, helpless head.   360

"And there from morn till twilight bound,
I felt the heavy hours toil round,
With just enough of life to see
My last of suns go down on me,
In hopeless certainty of mind,
That makes us feel at length resign'd
To that which our foreboding years
Present the worst and last of fears
Inevitable—even a boon,
Nor more unkind for coming soon,   370
Yet shunn'd and dreaded with such care,
As if it only were a snare
  That prudence might escape:
At times both wish'd for and implored,
At times sought with self-pointed sword,
Yet still a dark and hideous close
To even intolerable woes,
  And welcome in no shape.
And, strange to say, the sons of pleasure,
They who have revell'd beyond measure   380
In beauty, wassail, wine, and treasure,
Die calm, or calmer, oft than he
Whose heritage was misery:
For he who hath in turn run through
All that was beautiful and new,
  Hath nought to hope, and nought to leave;
And, save the future, (which is view'd

Not quite as men are base or good,
But as their nerves may be endued,)
  With nought perhaps to grieve : 390
The wretch still hopes his woes must end,
And Death, whom he should deem his friend,
Appears, to his distemper'd eyes,
Arrived to rob him of his prize,
The tree of his new Paradise.
To-morrow would have given him all,
Repaid his pangs, repair'd his fall ;
To-morrow would have been the first
Of days no more deplored or curst,
But bright, and long, and beckoning years, 400
Seen dazzling through the mist of tears,
Guerdon of many a painful hour ;
To-morrow would have given him power
To rule, to shine, to smite, to save—
And must it dawn upon his grave ?

X

"The sun was sinking—still I lay
  Chained to the chill and stiffening steed ;
I thought to mingle there our clay,
  And my dim eyes of death had need ;
  No hope arose of being freed : 410
I cast my last looks up the sky,
  And there between me and the sun
I saw the expecting raven fly,
Who scarce would wait till both should die,
  Ere his repast begun ;
He flew, and perch'd, then flew once more,
And each time nearer than before ;

I saw his wing through twilight flit,
And once so near me he alit
I could have smote, but lack'd the strength ;
But the slight motion of my hand,
And feeble scratching of the sand,
The exerted throat's faint struggling noise,
Which scarcely could be called a voice,
　　Together scared him off at length.
I know no more—my latest dream
　　Is something of a lovely star
　　Which fix'd my dull eyes from afar,
And went and came with wandering beam,
And of the cold, dull, swimming, dense
Sensation of recurring sense,
And then subsiding back to death,
And then again a little breath,
A little thrill, a short suspense,
　　An icy sickness curdling o'er
My heart, and sparks that cross'd my brain—
A gasp, a throb, a start of pain,
　　A sigh, and nothing more.

XI

" I woke—where was I ? Do I see
A human face look down on me ?
And doth a roof above me close ?
Do these limbs on a couch repose ?
Is this a chamber where I lie ?
And is it mortal yon bright eye,
That watches me with gentle glance ?
　　I closed my own again 'once more,

As doubtful that the former trance
  Could not as yet be o'er.
A slender girl, long-hair'd, and tall,
Sate watching by the cottage wall; 450
The sparkle of her eye I caught,
Even with my first return of thought:
For ever and anon she threw
  A prying, pitying glance on me
  With her black eyes so wild and free;
I gazed, and gazed, until I knew
  No vision it could be,—
But that I lived, and was released
From adding to the vulture's feast:
And when the Cossack maid beheld 460
My heavy eyes at length unseal'd,
She smiled—and I essay'd to speak,
  But fail'd—and she approach'd, and made
  With lip and finger signs that said,
I must not strive as yet to break
The silence, till my strength should be
Enough to leave my accents free;
And then her hand on mine she laid,
And smooth'd the pillow for my head,
And stole along on tiptoe tread, 470
  And gently oped the door, and spake
In whispers—ne'er was voice so sweet!
Even music follow'd her light feet:
  But those she call'd were not awake,
And she went forth; but, ere she pass'd,
Another look on me she cast,
  Another sign she made, to say,
That I had nought to fear, that all

Were near, at my command or call,
   And she would not delay
Her due return :—while she was gone,
Methought I felt too much alone.

XII

"She came with mother and with sire—
What need of more ?—I will not tire
With long recital of the rest,
Since I became the Cossack's guest.
They found me senseless on the plain,
   They bore me to the nearest hut,
They brought me into life again—
Me—one day o'er their realm to reign !
   Thus the vain fool who strove to glut
His rage, refining on my pain,
   Sent me forth to the wilderness,
Bound, naked, bleeding, and alone,
To pass the desert to a throne,—
   What mortal his own doom may guess ?
   Let none despond, let none despair !
To-morrow the Borysthenes
May see our coursers graze at ease
Upon his Turkish bank, and never
Had I such welcome for a river
   As I shall yield when safely there.
Comrades, good-night ! "—The Hetman threw
His length beneath the oak-tree shade,
   With leafy couch already made,
A bed nor comfortless nor new
To him, who took his rest whene'er

The hour arrived, no matter where :
  His eyes the hastening slumbers steep.
And if ye marvel Charles forgot
  To thank his tale, *he* wonder'd not,—
    The king had been an hour asleep.

JOHN KEATS

LAMIA

Part I

Upon a time, before the faery broods
Drove Nymph and Satyr from the prosperous woods,
Before King Oberon's bright diadem,
Sceptre, and mantle, clasp'd with dewy gem,
Frighted away the Dryads and the Fauns
From rushes green, and brakes, and cowslip'd lawns,
The ever-smitten Hermes empty left
His golden throne, bent warm on amorous theft:
From high Olympus had he stolen light,
On this side of Jove's clouds, to escape the sight   10
Of his great summoner, and made retreat
Into a forest on the shores of Crete.
For somewhere in that sacred island dwelt
A nymph, to whom all hoofed Satyrs knelt;
At whose white feet the languid Tritons poured
Pearls, while on land they wither'd and adored.
Fast by the springs where she to bathe was wont,
And in those meads where sometime she might haunt,
Were strewn rich gifts, unknown to any Muse,
Though Fancy's casket were unlock'd to choose.   20
Ah, what a world of love was at her feet!
So Hermes thought, and a celestial heat

Burnt from his winged heels to either ear,
That from a whiteness, as the lily clear,
Blush'd into roses 'mid his golden hair,
Fallen in jealous curls about his shoulders bare.
From vale to vale, from wood to wood, he flew,
Breathing upon the flowers his passion new,
And wound with many a river to its head,
To find where this sweet nymph prepar'd her secret
    bed: 30
In vain; the sweet nymph might nowhere be found,
And so he rested, on the lonely ground,
Pensive, and full of painful jealousies
Of the Wood-Gods, and even the very trees.
There as he stood, he heard a mournful voice,
Such as once heard, in gentle heart, destroys
All pain but pity: thus the lone voice spake:
' When from this wreathed tomb shall I awake!
When move in a sweet body fit for life,
And love, and pleasure, and the ruddy strife   40
Of hearts and lips! Ah, miserable me!'
The God, dove-footed, glided silently
Round bush and tree, soft-brushing, in his speed,
The taller grasses and full-flowering weed,
Until he found a palpitating snake,
Bright, and cirque-couchant in a dusky brake.

    She was a gordian shape of dazzling hue,
Vermilion-spotted, golden, green, and blue;
Striped like a zebra, freckled like a pard,
Eyed like a peacock, and all crimson barr'd;   50
And full of silver moons, that, as she breathed,
Dissolv'd, or brighter shone, or interwreathed

Their lustres with the gloomier tapestries—
So rainbow-sided, touch'd with miseries,
She seem'd, at once, some penanced lady elf,
Some demon's mistress, or the demon's self.
Upon her crest she wore a wannish fire
Sprinkled with stars, like Ariadne's tiar :
Her head was serpent, but ah, bitter-sweet !
She had a woman's mouth with all its pearls complete : 60
And for her eyes : what could such eyes do there
But weep, and weep, that they were born so fair ?
As Proserpine still weeps for her Sicilian air.
Her throat was serpent, but the words she spake
Came, as through bubbling honey, for Love's sake,
And thus ; while Hermes on his pinions lay,
Like a stoop'd falcon ere he takes his prey.

' Fair Hermes, crown'd with feathers, fluttering light,
I had a splendid dream of thee last night :
I saw thee sitting, on a throne of gold, 70
Among the Gods, upon Olympus old,
The only sad one ; for thou didst not hear
The soft, lute-finger'd Muses chaunting clear,
Nor even Apollo when he sang alone,
Deaf to his throbbing throat's long, long melodious moan.
I dreamt I saw thee, robed in purple flakes,
Break amorous through the clouds, as morning breaks,
And, swiftly as a bright Phœbean dart,
Strike for the Cretan isle ; and here thou art !
Too gentle Hermes, hast thou found the maid ? ' 80
Whereat the star of Lethe not delay'd
His rosy eloquence, and thus inquired :

'Thou smooth-lipp'd serpent, surely high inspired!
Thou beauteous wreath, with melancholy eyes,
Possess whatever bliss thou canst devise,
Telling me only where my nymph is fled,—
Where she doth breathe!' 'Bright planet, thou hast said,'
Return'd the snake, 'but seal with oaths, fair God!'
'I swear,' said Hermes, 'by my serpent rod,
And by thine eyes, and by thy starry crown!' 90
Light flew his earnest words, among the blossoms blown.
Then thus again the brilliance feminine:
'Too frail of heart! for this lost nymph of thine,
Free as the air, invisibly, she strays
About these thornless wilds; her pleasant days
She tastes unseen; unseen her nimble feet
Leave traces in the grass and flowers sweet;
From weary tendrils, and bow'd branches green,
She plucks the fruit unseen, she bathes unseen:
And by my power is her beauty veil'd 100
To keep it unaffronted, unassail'd
By the love-glances of unlovely eyes,
Of Satyrs, Fauns, and blear'd Silenus' sighs.
Pale grew her immortality, for woe
Of all these lovers, and she grieved so
I took compassion on her, bade her steep
Her hair in weird syrops, that would keep
Her loveliness invisible, yet free
To wander as she loves, in liberty.
Thou shalt behold her, Hermes, thou alone, 110
If thou wilt, as thou swearest, grant my boon!'
Then, once again, the charmed God began
An oath, and through the serpent's ears it ren

Warm, tremulous, devout, psalterian.
Ravish'd, she lifted her Circean head,
Blush'd a live damask, and swift-lisping said,
' I was a woman, let me have once more
A woman's shape, and charming as before.
I love a youth of Corinth—O the bliss !
Give me my woman's form, and place me where he is.   120
Stoop, Hermes, let me breathe upon thy brow,
And thou shalt see thy sweet nymph even now.'
The God on half-shut feathers sank serene,
She breath'd upon his eyes, and swift was seen
Of both the guarded nymph near-smiling on the green.
It was no dream ; or say a dream it was,
Real are the dreams of Gods, and smoothly pass
Their pleasures in a long immortal dream.
One warm, flush'd moment, hovering, it might seem
Dash'd by the wood-nymph's beauty, so he burn'd ;   130
Then, lighting on the printless verdure, turn'd
To the swoon'd serpent, and with languid arm,
Delicate, put to proof the lythe Caducean charm.
So done, upon the nymph his eyes he bent
Full of adoring tears and blandishment,
And towards her stept : she, like a moon in wane,
Faded before him, cower'd, nor could restrain
Her fearful sobs, self-folding like a flower
That faints into itself at evening hour :
But the God fostering her chilled hand,   140
She felt the warmth, her eyelids open'd bland,
And, like new flowers at morning song of bees,
Bloom'd, and gave up her honey to the lees.
Into the green-recessed woods they flew ;
Nor grew they pale, as mortal lovers do.

Left to herself, the serpent now began
To change ; her elfin blood in madness ran,
Her mouth foam'd, and the grass, therewith besprent,
Wither'd at dew so sweet and virulent ;
Her eyes in torture fix'd, and anguish drear,   150
Hot, glaz'd, and wide, with lid-lashes all sear,
Flash'd phosphor and sharp sparks, without one cooling
   tear.
The colours all inflam'd throughout her train,
She writh'd about, convuls'd with scarlet pain :
A deep volcanian yellow took the place
Of all her milder-mooned body's grace ;
And, as the lava ravishes the mead,
Spoilt all her silver mail, and golden brede ;
Made gloom of all her frecklings, streaks and bars,
Eclips'd her crescents, and lick'd up her stars :   160
So that, in moments few, she was undrest
Of all her sapphires, greens, and amethyst,
And rubious-argent : of all these bereft,
Nothing but pain and ugliness were left.
Still shone her crown ; that vanish'd, also she
Melted and disappear'd as suddenly ;
And in the air, her new voice luting soft,
Cried, ' Lycius ! gentle Lycius ! '—Borne aloft
With the bright mists about the mountains hoar
These words dissolv'd : Crete's forests heard no more. 170

  Whither fled Lamia, now a lady bright,
A full-born beauty new and exquisite ?
She fled into that valley they pass o'er
Who go to Corinth from Cenchreas' shore ;
And rested at the foot of those wild hills,

The rugged founts of the Peræan rills,
And of that other ridge whose barren back
Stretches, with all its mist and cloudy rack,
South-westward to Cleone. There she stood
About a young bird's flutter from a wood, 180
Fair, on a sloping green of mossy tread,
By a clear pool, wherein she passioned
To see herself escap'd from so sore ills,
While her robes flaunted with the daffodils.

   Ah, happy Lycius!—for she was a maid
More beautiful than ever twisted braid,
Or sigh'd, or blush'd, or on spring-flowered lea
Spread a green kirtle to the minstrelsy:
A virgin purest lipp'd, yet in the lore
Of love deep learned to the red heart's core: 190
Not one hour old, yet of sciential brain
To unperplex bliss from its neighbour pain;
Define their pettish limits, and estrange
Their points of contact, and swift counterchange;
Intrigue with the specious chaos, and dispart
Its most ambiguous atoms with sure art;
As though in Cupid's college she had spent
Sweet days a lovely graduate, still unshent,
And kept his rosy terms in idle languishment.

   Why this fair creature chose so fairily 200
By the wayside to linger, we shall see;
But first 'tis fit to tell how she could muse
And dream, when in the serpent prison-house,
Of all she list, strange or magnificent:
How, ever, where she will'd, her spirit went;

Whether to faint Elysium, or where
Down through tress-lifting waves the Nereids fair
Wind into Thetis' bower by many a pearly stair;
Or where God Bacchus drains his cups divine,
Stretch'd out, at ease, beneath a glutinous pine;   210
Or where in Pluto's gardens palatine
Mulciber's columns gleam in far piazzian line.
And sometimes into cities she would send
Her dream, with feast and rioting to blend;
And once, while among mortals dreaming thus,
She saw the young Corinthian Lycius
Charioting foremost in the envious race,
Like a young Jove with calm uneager face,
And fell into a swooning love of him.
Now on the moth-time of that evening dim   220
He would return that way, as well she knew,
To Corinth from the shore; for freshly blew
The eastern soft wind, and his galley now
Grated the quaystones with her brazen prow
In port Cenchreas, from Egina isle
Fresh anchor'd; whither he had been awhile
To sacrifice to Jove, whose temple there
Waits with high marble doors for blood and incense rare.
Jove heard his vows, and better'd his desire;
For by some freakful chance he made retire   230
From his companions, and set forth to walk,
Perhaps grown wearied of their Corinth talk:
Over the solitary hills he fared,
Thoughtless at first, but ere eve's star appeared
His phantasy was lost, where reason fades,
In the calm'd twilight of Platonic shades.
Lamia beheld him coming, near, more near—

Close to her passing, in indifference drear,
His silent sandals swept the mossy green;
So neighbour'd to him, and yet so unseen   240
She stood: he pass'd, shut up in mysteries,
His mind wrapp'd like his mantle, while her eyes
Follow'd his steps, and her neck regal white
Turn'd—syllabling thus, ' Ah, Lycius bright,
And will you leave me on the hills alone?
Lycius, look back! and be some pity shown.'
He did; not with cold wonder fearingly,
But Orpheus-like at an Eurydice;
For so delicious were the words she sung,
It seem'd he had lov'd them a whole summer long: 250
And soon his eyes had drunk her beauty up,
Leaving no drop in the bewildering cup,
And still the cup was full,—while he, afraid
Lest she should vanish ere his lip had paid
Due adoration, thus began to adore;
Her soft look growing coy, she saw his chain so sure:
' Leave thee alone! Look back! Ah, Goddess, see
Whether my eyes can ever turn from thee!
For pity do not this sad heart belie—
Even as thou vanishest so I shall die.   260
Stay! though a Naiad of the rivers, stay!
To thy far wishes will thy streams obey:
Stay! though the greenest woods be thy domain,
Alone they can drink up the morning rain:
Though a descended Pleiad, will not one
Of thine harmonious sisters keep in tune
Thy spheres, and as thy silver proxy shine?
So sweetly to these ravish'd ears of mine
Came thy sweet greeting, that if thou shouldst fade

Thy memory will waste me to a shade :— 270
For pity do not melt! '—' If I should stay,'
Said Lamia, ' here, upon this floor of clay,
And pain my steps upon these flowers too rough,
What canst thou say or do of charm enough
To dull the nice remembrance of my home?
Thou canst not ask me with thee here to roam
Over these hills and vales, where no joy is,—
Empty of immortality and bliss!
Thou art a scholar, Lycius, and must know
That finer spirits cannot breathe below 280
In human climes, and live : Alas! poor youth,
What taste of purer air hast thou to soothe
My essence? What serener palaces,
Where I may all my many senses please,
And by mysterious sleights a hundred thirsts appease?
It cannot be—Adieu!' So said, she rose
Tiptoe with white arms spread. He, sick to lose
The amorous promise of her lone complain,
Swoon'd, murmuring of love, and pale with pain.
The cruel lady, without any show 290
Of sorrow for her tender favourite's woe,
But rather, if her eyes could brighter be,
With brighter eyes and slow amenity,
Put her new lips to his, and gave afresh
The life she had so tangled in her mesh :
And as he from one trance was wakening
Into another, she began to sing,
Happy in beauty, life, and love, and every thing
A song of love, too sweet for earthly lyres,
While, like held breath, the stars drew in their panting
   fires. 300

And then she whisper'd in such trembling tone,
As those who, safe together met alone
For the first time through many anguish'd days,
Use other speech than looks ; bidding him raise
His drooping head, and clear his soul of doubt,
For that she was a woman, and without
Any more subtle fluid in her veins
Than throbbing blood, and that the self-same pains
Inhabited her frail-strung heart as his.
And next she wonder'd how his eyes could miss   310
Her face so long in Corinth, where, she said,
She dwelt but half retir'd, and there had led
Days happy as the gold coin could invent
Without the aid of love ; yet in content
Till she saw him, as once she pass'd him by,
Where 'gainst a column he leant thoughtfully
At Venus' temple porch, 'mid baskets heap'd
Of amorous herbs and flowers, newly reap'd
Late on that eve, as 'twas the night before
The Adonian feast ; whereof she saw no more,   320
But wept alone those days, for why should she adore ?
Lycius from death awoke into amaze,
To see her still, and singing so sweet lays ;
Then from amaze into delight he fell
To hear her whisper woman's lore so well ;
And every word she spake entic'd him on
To unperplex'd delight and pleasure known.
Let the mad poets say whate'er they please
Of the sweets of Fairies, Peris, Goddesses,
There is not such a treat among them all,   330
Haunters of cavern, lake, and waterfall,
As a real woman, lineal indeed

From Pyrrha's pebbles or old Adam's seed.
Thus gentle Lamia judg'd, and judg'd aright,
That Lycius could not love in half a fright,
So threw the goddess off, and won his heart
More pleasantly by playing woman's part,
With no more awe than what her beauty gave,
That, while it smote, still guaranteed to save.
Lycius to all made eloquent reply,   340
Marrying to every word a twinborn sigh;
And last, pointing to Corinth, ask'd her sweet,
If 'twas too far that night for her soft feet.
The way was short, for Lamia's eagerness
Made, by a spell, the triple league decrease
To a few paces; not at all surmised
By blinded Lycius, so in her comprized.
They pass'd the city gates, he knew not how,
So noiseless, and he never thought to know.

   As men talk in a dream, so Corinth all,   350
Throughout her palaces imperial,
And all her populous streets and temples lewd,
Mutter'd, like tempest in the distance brew'd,
To the wide-spreaded night above her towers.
Men, women, rich and poor, in the cool hours,
Shuffled their sandals o'er the pavement white,
Companion'd or alone; while many a light
Flared, here and there, from wealthy festivals,
And threw their moving shadows on the walls,
Or found them cluster'd in the corniced shade   360
Of some arch'd temple door, or dusky colonnade.

   Muffling his face, of greeting friends in fear,
Her fingers he press'd hard, as one came near

With curl'd gray beard, sharp eyes, and smooth bald
    crown,
Slow-stepp'd, and robed in philosophic gown :
Lycius shrank closer, as they met and past,
Into his mantle, adding wings to haste,
While hurried Lamia trembled : ' Ah,' said he,
' Why do you shudder, love, so ruefully ?
Why does your tender palm dissolve in dew ? '—   370
' I'm wearied,' said fair Lamia : ' tell me who
Is that old man ?   I cannot bring to mind
His features :—Lycius ! wherefore did you blind
Yourself from his quick eyes ? '   Lycius replied,
' 'Tis Apollonius sage, my trusty guide
And good instructor ; but to-night he seems
The ghost of folly haunting my sweet dreams.'

   While yet he spake they had arrived before
A pillar'd porch, with lofty portal door,
Where hung a silver lamp, whose phosphor glow   380
Reflected in the slabbed steps below,
Mild as a star in water ; for so new,
And so unsullied was the marble's hue,
So through the crystal polish, liquid fine,
Ran the dark veins, that none but feet divine
Could e'er have touch'd there.   Sounds Æolian
Breath'd from the hinges, as the ample span
Of the wide doors disclos'd a place unknown
Some time to any, but those two alone,
And a few Persian mutes, who that same year   390
Were seen about the markets : none knew where
They could inhabit ; the most curious
Were foil'd, who watch'd to trace them to their house :

And but the flitter-winged verse must tell,
For truth's sake, what woe afterwards befel,
'Twould humour many a heart to leave them thus,
Shut from the busy world of more incredulous.

Part II

Love in a hut, with water and a crust,
Is—Love, forgive us!—cinders, ashes, dust;
Love in a palace is perhaps at last
More grievous torment than a hermit's fast:—
That is a doubtful tale from faery land,
Hard for the non-elect to understand.
Had Lycius liv'd to hand his story down,
He might have given the moral a fresh frown,
Or clench'd it quite: but too short was their bliss
To breed distrust and hate, that make the soft voice hiss. 10
Besides, there, nightly, with terrific glare,
Love, jealous grown of so complete a pair,
Hover'd and buzz'd his wings, with fearful roar,
Above the lintel of their chamber door,
And down the passage cast a glow upon the floor.

For all this came a ruin: side by side
They were enthroned, in the eventide,
Upon a couch, near to a curtaining
Whose airy texture, from a golden string,
Floated into the room, and let appear 20
Unveil'd the summer heaven, blue and clear,
Betwixt two marble shafts:—there they reposed,
Where use had made it sweet, with eyelids closed,

Saving a tythe which love still open kept,
That they might see each other while they almost slept;
When from the slope side of a suburb hill,
Deafening the swallow's twitter, came a thrill
Of trumpets—Lycius started—the sounds fled,
But left a thought, a buzzing in his head.
For the first time, since first he harbour'd in 30
That purple-lined palace of sweet sin,
His spirit pass'd beyond its golden bourn
Into the noisy world almost forsworn.
The lady, ever watchful, penetrant,
Saw this with pain, so arguing a want
Of something more, more than her empery
Of joys ; and she began to moan and sigh
Because he mused beyond her, knowing well
That but a moment's thought is passion's passing bell.
' Why do you sigh, fair creature ? ' whisper'd he : 40
' Why do you think ? ' return'd she tenderly :
' You have deserted me ;—where am I now ?
Not in your heart while care weighs on your brow :
No, no, you have dismiss'd me ; and I go
From your breast houseless : ay, it must be so.'
He answer'd, bending to her open eyes,
Where he was mirror'd small in paradise,
' My silver planet, both of eve and morn !
Why will you plead yourself so sad forlorn,
While I am striving how to fill my heart 50
With deeper crimson, and a double smart ?
How to entangle, trammel up and snare
Your soul in mine, and labyrinth you there
Like the hid scent in an unbudded rose ?
Ay, a sweet kiss—you see your mighty woes.

My thoughts! shall I unveil them? Listen then!
What mortal hath a prize, that other men
May be confounded and abash'd withal,
But lets it sometimes pace abroad majestical,
And triumph, as in thee I should rejoice   60
Amid the hoarse alarm of Corinth's voice.
Let my foes choke, and my friends shout afar,
While through the thronged streets your bridal car
Wheels round its dazzling spokes.'—The lady's cheek
Trembled; she nothing said, but, pale and meek,
Arose and knelt before him, wept a rain
Of sorrows at his words; at last with pain
Beseeching him, the while his hand she wrung,
To change his purpose. He thereat was stung,
Perverse, with stronger fancy to reclaim   70
Her wild and timid nature to his aim :
Besides, for all his love, in self-despite,
Against his better self, he took delight
Luxurious in her sorrows, soft and new.
His passion, cruel grown, took on a hue
Fierce and sanguineous as 'twas possible
In one whose brow had no dark veins to swell.
Fine was the mitigated fury, like
Apollo's presence when in act to strike
The serpent—Ha, the serpent! certes, she   80
Was none. She burnt, she lov'd the tyranny,
And, all subdued, consented to the hour
When to the bridal he should lead his paramour.
Whispering in midnight silence, said the youth.
' Sure some sweet name thou hast, though, by my truth,
I have not ask'd it, ever thinking thee
Not mortal, but of heavenly progeny,

LAMIA

As still I do. Hast any mortal name,
Fit appellation for this dazzling frame ?
Or friends or kinsfolk on the citied earth,   90
To share our marriage feast and nuptial mirth ? '
' I have no friends,' said Lamia, ' no, not one ;
My presence in wide Corinth hardly known :
My parents' bones are in their dusty urns
Sepulchred, where no kindled incense burns,
Seeing all their luckless race are dead, save me,
And I neglect the holy rite for thee.
Even as you list invite your many guests ;
But if, as now it seems, your vision rests
With any pleasure on me, do not bid   100
Old Apollonius—from him keep me hid.'
Lycius, perplex'd at words so blind and blank,
Made close inquiry ; from whose touch she shrank,
Feigning a sleep ; and he to the dull shade
Of deep sleep in a moment was betray'd.

It was the custom then to bring away
The bride from home at blushing shut of day,
Veil'd, in a chariot, heralded along
By strewn flowers, torches, and a marriage song,
With other pageants : but this fair unknown   110
Had not a friend. So being left alone,
(Lycius was gone to summon all his kin)
And knowing surely she could never win
His foolish heart from its mad pompousness,
She set herself, high-thoughted, how to dress
The misery in fit magnificence.
She did so, but 'tis doubtful how and whence
Came, and who were her subtle servitors.

About the halls, and to and from the doors,
There was a noise of wings, till in short space 120
The glowing banquet-room shone with wide-arched grace.
A haunting music, sole perhaps and lone
Supportress of the faery-roof, made moan
Throughout, as fearful the whole charm might fade.
Fresh carved cedar, mimicking a glade
Of palm and plantain, met from either side,
High in the midst, in honour of the bride :
Two palms and then two plantains, and so on,
From either side their stems branch'd one to one
All down the aisled place ; and beneath all 130
There ran a stream of lamps straight on from wall to
    wall.
So canopied, lay an untasted feast
Teeming with odours. Lamia, regal drest,
Silently paced about, and as she went,
In pale contented sort of discontent,
Mission'd her viewless servants to enrich
The fretted splendour of each nook and niche.
Between the tree-stems, marbled plain at first,
Came jasper pannels ; then, anon, there burst
Forth creeping imagery of slighter trees, 140
And with the larger wove in small intricacies.
Approving all, she faded at self-will,
And shut the chamber up, close, hush'd and still,
Complete and ready for the revels rude,
When dreadful guests would come to spoil her solitude.

   The day appear'd, and all the gossip rout.
O senseless Lycius ! Madman ! wherefore flout
The silent-blessing fate, warm cloister'd hours,

And show to common eyes these secret bowers?
The herd approach'd ; each guest, with busy brain, 150
Arriving at the portal, gaz'd amain,
And enter'd marvelling : for they knew the street,
Remember'd it from childhood all complete
Without a gap, yet ne'er before had seen
That royal porch, that high-built fair demesne ;
So in they hurried all, maz'd, curious and keen :
Save one, who look'd thereon with eyes severe,
And with calm-planted steps walked in austere ;
'Twas Apollonius : something too he laugh'd,
As though some knotty problem, that had daft 160
His patient thought, had now begun to thaw,
And solve and melt :—'twas just as he foresaw.

   He met within the murmurous vestibule
His young disciple. ' 'Tis no common rule,
Lycius,' said he, ' for uninvited guest
To force himself upon you, and infest
With an unbidden presence the bright throng
Of younger friends ; yet must I do this wrong,
And you forgive me.' Lycius blush'd, and led
The old man through the inner doors broad-spread ; 170
With reconciling words and courteous mien
Turning into sweet milk the sophist's spleen.

   Of wealthy lustre was the banquet-room,
Fill'd with pervading brilliance and perfume :
Before each lucid pannel fuming stood
A censer fed with myrrh and spiced wood,
Each by a sacred tripod held aloft,
Whose slender feet wide-swerv'd upon the soft

Wool-woofed carpets : fifty wreaths of smoke
From fifty censers their light voyage took 180
To the high roof, still mimick'd as they rose
Along the mirror'd walls by twin-clouds odorous.
Twelve sphered tables, by silk seats insphered,
High as the level of a man's breast rear'd
On libbard's paws, upheld the heavy gold
Of cups and goblets, and the store thrice told
Of Ceres' horn, and, in huge vessels, wine
Came from the gloomy tun with merry shine.
Thus loaded with a feast the tables stood,
Each shrining in the midst the image of a God. 190

 When in an antichamber every guest
Had felt the cold full sponge to pleasure press'd,
By minist'ring slaves, upon his hands and feet,
And fragrant oils with ceremony meet
Pour'd on his hair, they all mov'd to the feast
In white robes, and themselves in order placed
Around the silken couches, wondering
Whence all this mighty cost and blaze of wealth could
 spring.

 Soft went the music the soft air along,
While fluent Greek a vowel'd undersong 200
Kept up among the guests, discoursing low
At first, for scarcely was the wine at flow ;
But when the happy vintage touch'd their brains,
Louder they talk, and louder come the strains
Of powerful instruments :—the gorgeous dyes,
The space, the splendour of the draperies,
The roof of awful richness, nectarous cheer,

Beautiful slaves, and Lamia's self, appear,
Now, when the wine has done its rosy deed,
And every soul from human trammels freed,   210
No more so strange ; for merry wine, sweet wine,
Will make Elysian shades not too fair, too divine.
Soon was God Bacchus at meridian height ;
Flush'd were their cheeks, and bright eyes double bright:
Garlands of every green, and every scent
From vales deflower'd, or forest-trees branch-rent,
In baskets of bright osier'd gold were brought
High as the handles heap'd, to suit the thought
Of every guest ; that each, as he did please,
Might fancy-fit his brows, silk-pillow'd at his ease.   220

 What wreath for Lamia ? What for Lycius ?
What for the sage, old Apollonius ?
Upon her aching forehead be there hung
The leaves of willow and of adder's tongue ;
And for the youth, quick, let us strip for him
The thyrsus, that his watching eyes may swim
Into forgetfulness ; and, for the sage,
Let spear-grass and the spiteful thistle wage
War on his temples. Do not all charms fly
At the mere touch of cold philosophy ?   230
There was an awful rainbow once in heaven :
We know her woof, her texture ; she is given
In the dull catalogue of common things.
Philosophy will clip an Angel's wings,
Conquer all mysteries by rule and line,
Empty the haunted air, and gnomed mine—
Unweave a rainbow, as it erewhile made
The tender-person'd Lamia melt into a shade.

By her glad Lycius sitting, in chief place,
Scarce saw in all the room another face, 240
Till, checking his love trance, a cup he took
Full brimm'd, and opposite sent forth a look
'Cross the broad table, to beseech a glance
From his old teacher's wrinkled countenance,
And pledge him. The bald-head philosopher
Had fix'd his eye, without a twinkle or stir
Full on the alarmed beauty of the bride,
Brow-beating her fair form, and troubling her sweet pride.
Lycius then press'd her hand, with devout touch,
As pale it lay upon the rosy couch: 250
'Twas icy, and the cold ran through his veins;
Then sudden it grew hot, and all the pains
Of an unnatural heat shot to his heart.
' Lamia, what means this? Wherefore dost thou start?
Know'st thou that man?' Poor Lamia answer'd not.
He gaz'd into her eyes, and not a jot
Own'd they the lovelorn piteous appeal:
More, more he gaz'd: his human senses reel:
Some hungry spell that loveliness absorbs;
There was no recognition in those orbs. 260
' Lamia!' he cried—and no soft-toned reply.
The many heard, and the loud revelry
Grew hush; the stately music no more breathes;
The myrtle sicken'd in a thousand wreaths.
By faint degrees, voice, lute, and pleasure ceased;
A deadly silence step by step increased,
Until it seem'd a horrid presence there,
And not a man but felt the terror in his hair.
' Lamia!' he shrieked; and nothing but the shriek
With its sad echo did the silence break. 270

'Begone, foul dream!' he cried, gazing again
In the bride's face, where now no azure vein
Wander'd on fair-spaced temples; no soft bloom
Misted the cheek; no passion to illume
The deep-recessed vision :—all was blight;
Lamia, no longer fair, there sat a deadly white.
'Shut, shut those juggling eyes, thou ruthless man!
Turn them aside, wretch! or the righteous ban
Of all the Gods, whose dreadful images
Here represent their shadowy presences,   280
May pierce them on the sudden with the thorn
Of painful blindness; leaving thee forlorn,
In trembling dotage to the feeblest fright
Of conscience, for their long offended might,
For all thine impious proud-heart sophistries,
Unlawful magic, and enticing lies.
Corinthians! look upon that gray-beard wretch!
Mark how, possess'd, his lashless eyelids stretch
Around his demon eyes! Corinthians, see!
My sweet bride withers at their potency.'   290
'Fool!' said the sophist, in an under-tone
Gruff with contempt; which a death-nighing moan
From Lycius answer'd, as heart-struck and lost
He sank supine beside the aching ghost.
'Fool! Fool!' repeated he, while his eyes still
Relented not, nor mov'd; 'from every ill
Of life have I preserved thee to this day,
And shall I see thee made a serpent's prey?'
Then Lamia breath'd death breath; the sophist's eye,
Like a sharp spear, went through her utterly,   300
Keen, cruel, perceant, stinging: she, as well
As her weak hand could any meaning tell,

Motion'd him to be silent ; vainly so,
He look'd and look'd again a level—No !
' A Serpent ! ' echoed he ; no sooner said,
Than with a frightful scream she vanished :
And Lycius' arms were empty of delight,
As were his limbs of life, from that same night.
On the high couch he lay !—his friends came round—
Supported him—no pulse, or breath they found, 310
And, in its marriage robe, the heavy body wound.

ALFRED LORD TENNYSON

THE HOLY GRAIL

FROM noiseful arms, and acts of prowess done
In tournament or tilt, Sir Percivale,
Whom Arthur and his knighthood call'd The Pure,
Had pass'd into the silent life of prayer,
Praise, fast, and alms ; and leaving for the cowl
The helmet in an abbey far away
From Camelot, there, and not long after, died.

And one, a fellow-monk among the rest,
Ambrosius, loved him much beyond the rest,
And honour'd him, and wrought into his heart 10
A way by love that waken'd love within,
To answer that which came : and as they sat
Beneath a world-old yew-tree, darkening half
The cloisters, on a gustful April morn
That puff'd the swaying branches into smoke
Above them, ere the summer when he died,
The monk Ambrosius question'd Percivale :

' O brother, I have seen this yew-tree smoke,
Spring after spring, for half a hundred years :
For never have I known the world without, 20
Nor ever stray'd beyond the pale : but thee,

When first thou camest—such a courtesy
Spake thro' the limbs and in the voice—I knew
For one of those who eat in Arthur's hall ;
For good ye are and bad, and like to coins,
Some true, some light, but every one of you
Stamp'd with the image of the King ; and now
Tell me, what drove thee from the Table Round,
My brother ? was it earthly passion crost ? '

' Nay,' said the knight ; ' for no such passion mine. 30
But the sweet vision of the Holy Grail
Drove me from all vainglories, rivalries,
And earthly heats that spring and sparkle out
Among us in the jousts, while women watch
Who wins, who falls ; and waste the spiritual strength
Within us, better offer'd up to Heaven.'

To whom the monk : ' The Holy Grail !—I trust
We are green in Heaven's eyes ; but here too much
We moulder—as to things without I mean—
Yet one of your own knights, a guest of ours, 40
Told us of this in our refectory,
But spake with such a sadness and so low
We heard not half of what he said. What is it ?
The phantom of a cup that comes and goes ? '

' Nay, monk ! what phantom ? ' answer'd Percivale.
' The cup, the cup itself, from which our Lord
Drank at the last sad supper with his own.
This, from the blessed land of Aromat—
After the day of darkness, when the dead
Went wandering o'er Moriah—the good saint 50

Arimathæan Joseph, journeying brought
To Glastonbury, where the winter thorn
Blossoms at Christmas, mindful of our Lord.
And there awhile it bode ; and if a man
Could touch or see it, he was heal'd at once,
By faith, of all his ills. But then the times
Grew to such evil that the holy cup
Was caught away to Heaven, and disappear'd.'

To whom the monk : ' From our old books I know
That Joseph came of old to Glastonbury,
And there the heathen Prince, Arviragus,
Gave him an isle of marsh whereon to build ;
And there he built with wattles from the marsh
A little lonely church in days of yore,
For so they say, these books of ours, but seem
Mute of this miracle, far as I have read.
But who first saw the holy thing to-day ? '

' A woman,' answered Percivale, ' a nun,
And one no further off in blood from me
Than sister ; and if ever holy maid
With knees of adoration wore the stone,
A holy maid ; tho' never maiden glow'd,
But that was in her earlier maidenhood,
With such a fervent flame of human love,
Which being rudely blunted, glanced and shot
Only to holy things ; to prayer and praise
She gave herself, to fast and alms. And yet,
Nun as she was, the scandal of the Court,
Sin against Arthur and the Table Round,
And the strange sound of an adulterous race,

Across the iron grating of her cell
Beat, and she pray'd and fasted all the more.

'And he to whom she told her sins, or what
Her all but utter whiteness held for sin,
A man wellnigh a hundred winters old,
Spake often with her of the Holy Grail,
A legend handed down thro' five or six,
And each of these a hundred winters old,
From our Lord's time. And when King Arthur made
His Table Round, and all men's hearts became   90
Clean for a season, surely he had thought
That now the Holy Grail would come again;
But sin broke out. Ah, Christ, that it would come,
And heal the world of all their wickedness!
'O Father!' ask'd the maiden, 'might it come,
To me by prayer and fasting?' 'Nay,' said he,
'I know not, for thy heart is pure as snow.'
And so she pray'd and fasted, till the sun
Shone, and the wind blew, thro' her, and I thought
She might have risen and floated when I saw her.   100

'For on a day she sent to speak with me.
And when she came to speak, behold her eyes
Beyond my knowing of them, beautiful,
Beyond all knowing of them, wonderful,
Beautiful in the light of holiness.
And "O my brother Percivale," she said,
"Sweet brother, I have seen the Holy Grail:
For, waked at dead of night, I heard a sound
As of a silver horn from o'er the hills
Blown, and I thought, 'It is not Arthur's use   110

To hunt by moonlight ; ' and the slender sound
As from a distance beyond distance grew
Coming upon me—O never harp nor horn,
Nor aught we blow with breath, or touch with hand,
Was like that music as it came ; and then
Stream'd thro' my cell a cold and silver beam,
And down the long beam stole the Holy Grail,
Rose-red with beatings in it, as if alive,
Till all the white walls of my cell were dyed
With rosy colours leaping on the wall ; 120
And then the music faded, and the Grail
Past, and the beam decay'd, and from the walls
The rosy quiverings died into the night.
So now the Holy Thing is here again
Among us, brother, fast thou too and pray,
And tell thy brother knights to fast and pray,
That so perchance the vision may be seen
By thee and those, and all the world be heal'd."

' Then leaving the pale nun, I spake of this
To all men ; and myself fasted and pray'd 130
Always, and many among us many a week
Fasted and pray'd even to the uttermost,
Expectant of the wonder that would be.

' And one there was among us, ever moved
Among us in white armour, Galahad.
" God make thee good as thou art beautiful,"
Said Arthur, when he dubb'd him knight ; and none,
In so young youth, was ever made a knight
Till Galahad ; and this Galahad, when he heard
My sister's vision, fill'd me with amaze ; 140

His eyes became so like her own, they seem'd
Hers, and himself her brother more than I.

 ' Sister or brother none had he ; but some
Call'd him a son of Lancelot, and some said
Begotten by enchantment—chatterers they,
Like birds of passage piping up and down,
That gape for flies—we know not whence they come ;
For when was Lancelot wanderingly lewd ?

 ' But she, the wan sweet maiden, shore away
Clean from her forehead all that wealth of hair   150
Which made a silken mat-work for her feet ;
And out of this she plaited broad and long
A strong sword-belt, and wove with silver thread
And crimson in the belt a strange device,
A crimson grail within a silver beam ;
And saw the bright boy-knight, and bound it on him,
Saying, " My knight, my love, my knight of heaven,
O thou, my love, whose love is one with mine,
I, maiden, round thee, maiden, bind my belt.
Go forth, for thou shalt see what I have seen,   160
And break thro' all, till one will crown thee king
Far in the spiritual city ; " and as she spake
She sent the deathless passion in her eyes
Thro' him, and made him hers, and laid her mind
On him, and he believed in her belief.

 ' Then came a year of miracle : O brother,
In our great hall there stood a vacant chair,
Fashion'd by Merlin ere he past away,
And carven with strange figures ; and in and out

The figures, like a serpent, ran a scroll 170
Of letters in a tongue no man could read.
And Merlin call'd it " The Siege perilous,"
Perilous for good and ill ; " for there," he said,
" No man could sit but he should lose himself : "
And once by misadvertence Merlin sat
In his own chair, and so was lost ; but he,
Galahad, when he heard of Merlin's doom,
Cried, " If I lose myself, I save myself ! "

' Then on a summer night it came to pass,
While the great banquet lay along the hall, 180
That Galahad would sit down in Merlin's chair.

' And all at once, as there we sat, we heard
A cracking and a riving of the roofs,
And rending, and a blast, and overhead
Thunder, and in the thunder was a cry.
And in the blast there smote along the hall
A beam of light seven times more clear than day :
And down the long beam stole the Holy Grail
All over cover'd with a luminous cloud,
And none might see who bare it, and it past. 190
But every knight beheld his fellow's face
As in a glory, and all the knights arose,
And staring each at other like dumb men
Stood, till I found a voice and sware a vow.

' I sware a vow before them all, that I,
Because I had not seen the Grail, would ride
A twelvemonth and a day in quest of it,
Until I found and saw it, as the nun

My sister saw it; and Galahad sware the vow,
And good Sir Bors, our Lancelot's cousin, sware,   200
And Lancelot sware, and many among the knights,
And Gawain sware, and louder than the rest.'

Then spake the monk Ambrosius, asking him,
' What said the King ? Did Arthur take the vow ? '

' Nay, for my lord,' said Percivale, ' the King,
Was not in hall : for early that same day,
Scaped thro' a cavern from a bandit hold,
An outraged maiden sprang into the hall
Crying on help : for all her shining hair
Was smear'd with earth, and either milky arm   210
Red-rent with hooks of bramble, and all she wore
Torn as a sail that leaves the rope is torn
In tempest : so the King arose and went
To smoke the scandalous hive of those wild bees
That made such honey in his realm. Howbeit
Some little of this marvel he too saw,
Returning o'er the plain that then began
To darken under Camelot ; whence the King
Look'd up, calling aloud, " Lo, there ! the roofs
Of our great hall are roll'd in thunder-smoke !   220
Pray Heaven, they be not smitten by the bolt."
For dear to Arthur was that hall of ours,
As having there so oft with all his knights
Feasted, and as the stateliest under heaven.

' O brother, had you known our mighty hall,
Which Merlin built for Arthur long ago !
For all the sacred mount of Camelot,

And all the dim rich city, roof by roof,
Tower after tower, spire beyond spire,
By grove, and garden-lawn, and rushing brook,   230
Climbs to the mighty hall that Merlin built.
And four great zones of sculpture, set betwixt
With many a mystic symbol, gird the hall :
And in the lowest beasts are slaying men,
And in the second men are slaying beasts,
And on the third are warriors, perfect men,
And on the fourth are men with growing wings,
And over all one statue in the mould
Of Arthur, made by Merlin, with a crown,
And peak'd wings pointed to the Northern Star.   240
And eastward fronts the statue, and the crown
And both the wings are made of gold, and flame
At sunrise till the people in far fields,
Wasted so often by the heathen hordes,
Behold it, crying, " We have still a King."

'And, brother, had you known our hall within,
Broader and higher than any in all the lands !
Where twelve great windows blazon Arthur's wars,
And all the light that falls upon the board
Streams thro' the twelve great battles of our King.   250
Nay, one there is, and at the eastern end,
Wealthy with wandering lines of mount and mere,
Where Arthur finds the brand Excalibur.
And also one to the west, and counter to it,
And blank : and who shall blazon it ? when and
    how ?—
O there, perchance, when all our wars are done,
The brand Excalibur will be cast away.

'So to this hall full quickly rode the King,
In horror lest the work by Merlin wrought,
Dreamlike, should on the sudden vanish, wrapt   260
In unremorseful folds of rolling fire.
And in he rode, and up I glanced, and saw
The golden dragon sparkling over all :
And many of those who burnt the hold, their arms
Hack'd, and their foreheads grimed with smoke, and sear'd,
Follow'd, and in among bright faces, ours,
Full of the vision, prest : and then the King
Spake to me, being nearest, " Percivale,"
(Because the hall was all in tumult—some
Vowing, and some protesting), " what is this ? "   270

' O brother, when I told him what had chanced,
My sister's vision, and the rest, his face
Darken'd, as I have seen it more than once,
When some brave deed seem'd to be done in vain,
Darken ; and " Woe is me, my knights," he cried,
" Had I been here, ye had not sworn the vow."
Bold was mine answer, " Had thyself been here,
My King, thou wouldst have sworn."   " Yea, yea," said he,
" Art thou so bold and hast not seen the Grail ? "

' " Nay, lord, I heard the sound, I saw the light,   280
But since I did not see the Holy Thing,
I sware a vow to follow it till I saw."

' Then when he ask'd us, knight by knight, if any
Had seen it, all their answers were as one :
" Nay, lord, and therefore have we sworn our vows."

' " Lo now," said Arthur, " have ye seen a cloud ?
What go ye into the wilderness to see ? "

' Then Galahad on the sudden, and in a voice
Shrilling along the hall to Arthur, call'd,
" But I, Sir Arthur, saw the Holy Grail, 290
I saw the Holy Grail and heard a cry—
' O Galahad, and O Galahad, follow me.' "

' " Ah, Galahad, Galahad," said the King, " for such
As thou art is the vision, not for these.
Thy holy nun and thou have seen a sign—
Holier is none, my Percivale, than she—
A sign to maim this Order which I made.
But ye, that follow but the leader's bell "
(Brother, the King was hard upon his knights)
" Taliessin is our fullest throat of song, 300
And one hath sung and all the dumb will sing.
Lancelot is Lancelot, and hath overborne
Five knights at once, and every younger knight,
Unproven, holds himself as Lancelot,
Till overborne by one, he learns—and ye,
What are ye ? Galahads ?—no, nor Percivales "
(For thus it pleased the King to range me close
After Sir Galahad) ; " nay," said he, " but men
With strength and will to right the wrong'd, of power
To lay the sudden heads of violence flat, 310
Knights that in twelve great battles splash'd and dyed
The strong White Horse in his own heathen blood—
But one hath seen, and all the blind will see.
Go, since your vows are sacred, being made :
Yet—for ye know the cries of all my realm

Pass thro' this hall—how often, O my knights,
Your places being vacant at my side,
This chance of noble deeds will come and go
Unchallenged, while ye follow wandering fires
Lost in the quagmire! Many of you, yea most, 320
Return no more: ye think I show myself
Too dark a prophet: come now, let us meet
The morrow morn once more in one full field
Of gracious pastime, that once more the King,
Before ye leave him for this Quest, may count
The yet-unbroken strength of all his knights,
Rejoicing in that Order which he made."

'So when the sun broke next from underground,
All the great table of our Arthur closed
And clash'd in such a tourney and so full, 330
So many lances broken—never yet
Had Camelot seen the like, since Arthur came;
And I myself and Galahad, for a strength
Was in us from the vision, overthrew
So many knights that all the people cried,
And almost burst the barriers in their heat,
Shouting, "Sir Galahad and Sir Percivale!"

'But when the next day brake from underground—
O brother, had you known our Camelot,
Built by old kings, age after age, so old 340
The King himself had fears that it would fall,
So strange, and rich, and dim; for where the roofs
Totter'd toward each other in the sky,
Met foreheads all along the street of those
Who watch'd us pass; and lower, and where the long

Rich galleries, lady-laden, weigh'd the necks
Of dragons clinging to the crazy walls,
Thicker than drops from thunder, showers of flowers
Fell as we past; and men and boys astride
On wyvern, lion, dragon, griffin, swan,   350
At all the corners, named us each by name,
Calling " God speed ! " but in the ways below
The knights and ladies wept, and rich and poor
Wept, and the King himself could hardly speak
For grief, and all in middle street the Queen,
Who rode by Lancelot, wail'd and shriek'd aloud,
" This madness has come on us for our sins."
So to the Gate of the three Queens we came,
Where Arthur's wars are render'd mystically,
And thence departed every one his way.   360

  ' And I was lifted up in heart, and thought
Of all my late-shown prowess in the lists,
How my strong lance had beaten down the knights,
So many and famous names ; and never yet
Had heaven appear'd so blue, nor earth so green,
For all my blood danced in me, and I knew
That I should light upon the Holy Grail.

  ' Thereafter, the dark warning of our King,
That most of us would follow wandering fires,
Came like a driving gloom across my mind.   370
Then every evil word I had spoken once,
And every evil thought I had thought of old,
And every evil deed I ever did,
Awoke and cried, " This Quest is not for thee."
And lifting up mine eyes, I found myself

Alone, and in a land of sand and thorns,
And I was thirsty even unto death;
And I, too, cried, "This Quest is not for thee."

' And on I rode, and when I thought my thirst
Would slay me, saw deep lawns, and then a brook, 380
With one sharp rapid, where the crisping white
Play'd ever back upon the sloping wave,
And took both ear and eye; and o'er the brook
Were apple-trees, and apples by the brook
Fallen, and on the lawns. "I will rest here,"
I said, "I am not worthy of the Quest;"
But even while I drank the brook, and ate
The goodly apples, all these things at once
Fell into dust, and I was left alone,
And thirsting, in a land of sand and thorns. 390

' And then behold a woman at a door
Spinning; and fair the house whereby she sat,
And kind the woman's eyes and innocent,
And all her bearing gracious; and she rose
Opening her arms to meet me, as who should say,
"Rest here;" but when I touch'd her, lo! she, too,
Fell into dust and nothing, and the house
Became no better than a broken shed,
And in it a dead babe; and also this
Fell into dust, and I was left alone. 400

' And on I rode, and greater was my thirst.
Then flash'd a yellow gleam across the world,
And where it smote the plowshare in the field,
The plowman left his plowing, and fell down

THE HOLY GRAIL

Before it; where it glitter'd on her pail;
The milkmaid left her milking, and fell down
Before it, and I knew not why, but thought
" The sun is rising," tho' the sun had risen.
Then was I ware of one that on me moved
In golden armour with a crown of gold 410
About a casque all jewels; and his horse
In golden armour jewell'd everywhere:
And on the splendour came, flashing me blind;
And seem'd to me the Lord of all the world,
Being so huge. But when I thought he meant
To crush me, moving on me, lo! he, too,
Open'd his arms to embrace me as he came,
And up I went and touch'd him, and he, too,
Fell into dust, and I was left alone
And wearying in a land of sand and thorns. 420

' And I rode on and found a mighty hill,
And on the top, a city wall'd: the spires
Prick'd with incredible pinnacles into heaven.
And by the gateway stirr'd a crowd; and these
Cried to me climbing, " Welcome, Percivale!
Thou mightiest and thou purest among men!"
And glad was I and clomb, but found at top
No man, nor any voice. And thence I past
Far thro' a ruinous city, and I saw
That man had once dwelt there; but there I found 430
Only one man of an exceeding age.
" Where is that goodly company," said I,
" That so cried out upon me?" and he had
Scarce any voice to answer, and yet gasp'd,
" Whence and what art tnou?" and even as he spoke

Fell into dust, and disappear'd, and I
Was left alone once more, and cried in grief,
" Lo, if I find the Holy Grail itself
And touch it, it will crumble into dust."

' And thence I dropt into a lowly vale, 440
Low as the hill was high, and where the vale
Was lowest, found a chapel, and thereby
A holy hermit in a hermitage,
To whom I told my phantoms, and he said :
' " O son, thou hast not true humility,
The highest virtue, mother of them all ;
For when the Lord of all things made Himself
Naked of glory for His mortal change,
' Take thou my robe,' she said, ' for all is thine,'
And all her form shone forth with sudden light 450
So that the angels were amazed, and she
Follow'd Him down, and like a flying star
Led on the gray-hair'd wisdom of the east ;
But her thou hast not known : for what is this
Thou thoughtest of thy prowess and thy sins ?
Thou hast not lost thyself to save thyself
As Galahad."   When the hermit made an end,
In silver armour suddenly Galahad shone
Before us, and against the chapel door
Laid lance, and enter'd, and we knelt in prayer. 460
And there the hermit slaked my burning thirst,
And at the sacring of the mass I saw
The holy elements alone ; but he,
" Saw ye no more ?   I, Galahad, saw the Grail,
The Holy Grail, descend upon the shrine :
I saw the fiery face as of a child

That smote itself into the bread, and went;
And hither am I come; and never yet
Hath what thy sister taught me first to see,
This Holy Thing, fail'd from my side, nor come   470
Cover'd, but moving with me night and day,
Fainter by day, but always in the night
Blood-red, and sliding down the blacken'd marsh
Blood-red, and on the naked mountain top
Blood-red, and in the sleeping mere below
Blood-red. And in the strength of this I rode,
Shattering all evil customs everywhere,
And past thro' Pagan realms, and made them mine,
And clash'd with Pagan hordes, and bore them down,
And broke thro' all, and in the strength of this   480
Come victor. But my time is hard at hand,
And hence I go: and one will crown me king
Far in the spiritual city; and come thou, too,
For thou shalt see the vision when I go."

'While thus he spake, his eye, dwelling on mine,
Drew me, with power upon me, till I grew
One with him, to believe as he believed.
Then, when the day began to wane, we went.

'There rose a hill that none but man could climb,
Scarr'd with a hundred wintry water-courses—   490
Storm at the top, and when we gain'd it, storm
Round us and death; for every moment glanced
His silver arms and gloom'd: so quick and thick
The lightnings here and there to left and right
Struck, till the dry old trunks about us, dead,
Yea, rotten with a hundred years of death,

Sprang into fire ; and at the base we found
On either hand, as far as eye could see,
A great black swamp and of an evil smell,
Part black, part whiten'd with the bones of men,   500
Not to be crost, save that some ancient king
Had built a way, where, link'd with many a bridge,
A thousand piers ran into the great Sea.
And Galahad fled along them bridge by bridge,
And every bridge as quickly as he crost
Sprang into fire and vanish'd, tho' I yearn'd
To follow : and thrice above him all the heavens
Open'd and blazed with thunder such as seem'd
Shoutings of all the sons of God : and first
At once I saw him far on the great Sea,   510
In silver-shining armour starry-clear ;
And o'er his head the Holy Vessel hung
Clothed in white samite or a luminous cloud.
And with exceeding swiftness ran the boat,
If boat it were—I saw not whence it came.
And when the heavens open'd and blazed again
Roaring, I saw him like a silver star—
And had he set the sail, or had the boat
Become a living creature clad with wings ?
And o'er his head the Holy Vessel hung   520
Redder than any rose, a joy to me,
For now I knew the veil had been withdrawn.
Then in a moment when they blazed again
Opening, I saw the least of little stars
Down on the waste, and straight beyond the star
I saw the spiritual city and all her spires
And gateways in a glory like one pearl—
No larger, tho' the goal of all the saints—

Strike from the sea ; and from the star there shot
A rose-red sparkle to the city, and there   530
Dwelt, and I knew it was the Holy Grail,
Which never eyes on earth again shall see.
Then fell the floods of heaven drowning the deep.
And how my feet recrost the deathful ridge
No memory in me lives ; but that I touch'd
The chapel-doors at dawn I know ; and thence
Taking my war-horse from the holy man,
Glad that no phantom vext me more, return'd
To whence I came, the gate of Arthur's wars.'

' O brother,' ask'd Ambrosius,—' for in sooth   540
These ancient books—and they would win thee—teem,
Only I find not there this Holy Grail,
With miracles and marvels like to these,
Not all unlike ; which oftentime I read,
Who read but on my breviary with ease,
Till my head swims ; and then go forth and pass
Down to the little thorpe that lies so close,
And almost plaster'd like a martin's nest
To these old walls—and mingle with our folk ;
And knowing every honest face of theirs   550
As well as ever shepherd knew his sheep,
And every homely secret in their hearts,
Delight myself with gossip and old wives,
And ills and aches, and teethings, lyings-in,
And mirthful sayings, children of the place,
That have no meaning half a league away :
Or lulling random squabbles when they rise,
Chafferings and chatterings at the market-cross,
Rejoice, small man, in this small world of mine,

Yea, even in their hens and in their eggs— 560
O brother, saving this Sir Galahad,
Came ye on none but phantoms in your quest,
No man, no woman?'

                Then Sir Percivale :
'All men, to one so bound by such a vow,
And women were as phantoms. O, my brother,
Why wilt thou shame me to confess to thee
How far I falter'd from my quest and vow?
For after I had lain so many nights,
A bedmate of the snail and eft and snake,
In grass and burdock, I was changed to wan 570
And meagre, and the vision had not come ;
And then I chanced upon a goodly town
With one great dwelling in the middle of it ;
Thither I made, and there was I disarm'd
By maidens each as fair as any flower :
But when they led me into hall, behold,
The Princess of that castle was the one,
Brother, and that one only, who had ever
Made my heart leap ; for when I moved of old
A slender page about her father's hall, 580
And she a slender maiden, all my heart
Went after her with longing : yet we twain
Had never kiss'd a kiss, or vow'd a vow.
And now I came upon her once again,
And one had wedded her, and he was dead,
And all his land and wealth and state were hers.
And while I tarried, every day she set
A banquet richer than the day before
By me ; for all her longing and her will

Was toward me as of old ; till one fair morn,　　590
I walking to and fro beside a stream
That flash'd across her orchard underneath
Her castle-walls, she stole upon my walk,
And calling me the greatest of all knights,
Embraced me, and so kiss'd me the first time,
And gave herself and all her wealth to me.
Then I remember'd Arthur's warning word,
That most of us would follow wandering fires,
And the Quest faded in my heart. Anon,
The heads of all her people drew to me,　　600
With supplication both of knees and tongue :
" We have heard of thee : thou art our greatest knight,
Our Lady says it, and we well believe :
Wed thou our Lady, and rule over us,
And thou shalt be as Arthur in our land."
O me, my brother ! but one night my vow
Burnt me within, so that I rose and fled,
But wail'd and wept, and hated mine own self,
And ev'n the Holy Quest, and all but her ;
Then after I was join'd with Galahad　　610
Cared not for her, nor anything upon earth.'

　　Then said the monk, ' Poor men, when yule is cold,
Must be content to sit by little fires.
And this am I, so that ye care for me
Ever so little ; yea, and blest be Heaven
That brought thee here to this poor house of ours
Where all the brethren are so hard, to warm
My cold heart with a friend : but O the pity
To find thine own first love once more—to hold,
Hold her a wealthy bride within thine arms,　　620

Or all but hold, and then—cast her aside,
Forgoing all her sweetness, like a weed.
For we that want the warmth of double life,
We that are plagued with dreams of something sweet
Beyond all sweetness in a life so rich—
Ah, blessed Lord, I speak too earthlywise,
Seeing I never stray'd beyond the cell,
But live like an old badger in his earth,
With earth about him everywhere, despite
All fast and penance. Saw ye none beside,   630
None of your knights?'

'Yea so,' said Percivale:
'One night my pathway swerving east, I saw
The pelican on the casque of our Sir Bors
All in the middle of the rising moon:
And toward him spurr'd, and hail'd him, and he me,
And each made joy of either; then he ask'd,
" Where is he? hast thou seen him—Lancelot?—Once,"
Said good Sir Bors, " he dash'd across me —mad,
And maddening what he rode: and when I cried,
'Ridest thou then so hotly on a quest   640
So holy,' Lancelot shouted, ' Stay me not!
I have been the sluggard, and I ride apace,
For now there is a lion in the way.'
So vanished."

' Then Sir Bors had ridden on
Softly, and sorrowing for our Lancelot,
Because his former madness, once the talk
And scandal of our table, had return'd;
For Lancelot's kith and kin so worship him

That ill to him is ill to them ; to Bors
Beyond the rest : he well had been content   650
Not to have seen, so Lancelot might have seen,
The Holy Cup of healing ; and, indeed,
Being so clouded with his grief and love,
Small heart was his after the Holy Quest :
If God would send the vision, well : if not,
The Quest and he were in the hands of Heaven.

' And then, with small adventure met, Sir Bors
Rode to the lonest tract of all the realm,
And found a people there among their crags,
Our race and blood, a remnant that were left   660
Paynim amid their circles, and the stones
They pitch up straight to heaven : and their wise men
Were strong in that old magic which can trace
The wandering of the stars, and scoff'd at him
And this high Quest as at a simple thing :
Told him he follow'd—almost Arthur's words—
A mocking fire : " what other fire than he,
Whereby the blood beats, and the blossom blows,
And the sea rolls, and all the world is warm'd ? "
And when his answer chafed them, the rough crowd, 670
Hearing he had a difference with their priests,
Seized him, and bound and plunged him into a cell
Of great piled stones ; and lying bounden there
In darkness thro' innumerable hours
He heard the hollow-ringing heavens sweep
Over him till by miracle—what else ?—
Heavy as it was, a great stone slipt and fell,
Such as no wind could move : and thro' the gap
Glimmer'd the streaming scud : then came a night

Still as the day was loud ; and thro' the gap　　　680
The seven clear stars of Arthur's Table Round—
For, brother, so one night, because they roll
Thro' such a round in heaven, we named the stars,
Rejoicing in ourselves and in our King—
And these, like bright eyes of familiar friends,
In on him shone : " And then to me, to me,"
Said good Sir Bors, " beyond all hopes of mine,
Who scarce had pray'd or ask'd it for myself—
Across the seven clear stars—O grace to me—
In colour like the fingers of a hand　　　690
Before a burning taper, the sweet Grail
Glided and past, and close upon it peal'd
A sharp quick thunder." Afterwards, a maid,
Who kept our holy faith among her kin
In secret, entering, loosed and let him go.'

To whom the monk : ' And I remember now
That pelican on the casque : Sir Bors it was
Who spake so low and sadly at our board ;
And mighty reverent at our grace was he :
A square-set man and honest ; and his eyes,　　　700
An out-door sign of all the warmth within,
Smiled with his lips—a smile beneath a cloud,
But heaven had meant it for a sunny one :
Ay, ay, Sir Bors, who else ? But when ye reach'd
The city, found ye all your knights return'd,
Or was there sooth in Arthur's prophecy,
Tell me, and what said each, and what the King ? '
Then answer'd Percivale : ' And that can I,
Brother, and truly ; since the living words
Of so great men as Lancelot and our King　　　710

Pass not from door to door and out again,
But sit within the house. O, when we reach'd
The city, our horses stumbling as they trode
On heaps of ruin, hornless unicorns,
Crack'd basilisks, and splinter'd cockatrices,
And shatter'd talbots, which had left the stones
Raw, that they fell from, brought us to the hall.

' And there sat Arthur on the daïs-throne,
And those that had gone out upon the Quest,
Wasted and worn, and but a tithe of them,   720
And those that had not, stood before the King,
Who, when he saw me, rose, and bad me hail,
Saying, " A welfare in thine eye reproves
Our fear of some disastrous chance for thee
On hill, or plain, at sea, or flooding ford.
So fierce a gale made havoc here of late
Among the strange devices of our kings;
Yea, shook this newer, stronger hall of ours,
And from the statue Merlin moulded for us
Half-wrench'd a golden wing; but now—the Quest,   730
This vision—hast thou seen the Holy Cup,
That Joseph brought of old to Glastonbury?"

' So when I told him all thyself hast heard,
Ambrosius, and my fresh but fixt resolve
To pass away into the quiet life,
He answer'd not, but, sharply turning, ask'd
Of Gawain, " Gawain, was this Quest for thee?"

' " Nay, lord," said Gawain, " not for such as I.
Therefore I communed with a saintly man,
Who made me sure the Quest was not for me;   740

For I was much awearied of the Quest:
But found a silk pavilion in a field,
And merry maidens in it; and then this gale
Tore my pavilion from the tenting-pin,
And blew my merry maidens all about
With all discomfort; yea, and but for this,
My twelvemonth and a day were pleasant to me."

' He ceased; and Arthur turn'd to whom at first
He saw not, for Sir Bors, on entering, push'd
Athwart the throng to Lancelot, caught his hand,   750
Held it, and there, half-hidden by him, stood,
Until the King espied him, saying to him,
" Hail, Bors! if ever loyal man and true
Could see it, thou hast seen the Grail;" and Bors,
" Ask me not, for I may not speak of it:
I saw it;" and the tears were in his eyes.

' Then there remain'd but Lancelot, for the rest
Spake but of sundry perils in the storm;
Perhaps, like him of Cana in Holy Writ,
Our Arthur kept his best until the last;   760
" Thou, too, my Lancelot," ask'd the King, " my friend,
Our mightiest, hath this Quest avail'd for thee?"

' " Our mightiest!" answered Lancelot, with a groan;
" O King!"—and when he paused, methought I spied
A dying fire of madness in his eyes—
" O King, my friend, if friend of thine I be,
Happier are those that welter in their sin,
Swine in the mud, that cannot see for slime,
Slime of the ditch: but in me lived a sin
So strange, of such a kind, that all of pure,   770

Noble, and knightly in me twined and clung
Round that one sin, until the wholesome flower
And poisonous grew together, each as each,
Not to be pluck'd asunder ; and when thy knights
Sware, I sware with them only in the hope
That could I touch or see the Holy Grail
They might be pluck'd asunder. Then I spake
To one most holy saint, who wept and said,
That save they could be pluck'd asunder, all
My quest were but in vain ; to whom I vow'd 780
That I would work according as he will'd.
And forth I went, and while I yearn'd and strove
To tear the twain asunder in my heart,
My madness came upon me as of old,
And whipt me into waste fields far away ;
There was I beaten down by little men,
Mean knights, to whom the moving of my sword
And shadow of my spear had been enow
To scare them from me once ; and then I came
All in my folly to the naked shore, 790
Wide flats, where nothing but coarse grasses grew ;
But such a blast, my King, began to blow,
So loud a blast along the shore and sea,
Ye could not hear the waters for the blast,
Tho' heapt in mounds and ridges all the sea
Drove like a cataract, and all the sand
Swept like a river, and the clouded heavens
Were shaken with the motion and the sound.
And blackening in the sea-foam sway'd a boat,
Half-swallow'd in it, anchor'd with a chain ; 800
And in my madness to myself I said,
' I will embark and I will lose myself,

And in the great sea wash away my sin.'
I burst the chain, I sprang into the boat.
Seven days I drove along the dreary deep,
And with me drove the moon and all the stars;
And the wind fell, and on the seventh night
I heard the shingle grinding in the surge,
And felt the boat shock earth, and looking up,
Behold, the enchanted towers of Carbonek, 810
A castle like a rock upon a rock,
With chasm-like portals open to the sea,
And steps that met the breaker! there was none
Stood near it but a lion on each side
That kept the entry, and the moon was full.
Then from the boat I leapt, and up the stairs.
There drew my sword. With sudden-flaring manes
Those two great beasts rose upright like a man,
Each gript a shoulder, and I stood between;
And, when I would have smitten them, heard a voice, 820
' Doubt not, go forward; if thou doubt, the beasts
Will tear thee piecemeal.' Then with violence
The sword was dash'd from out my hand, and fell.
And up into the sounding hall I past;
But nothing in the sounding hall I saw,
No bench nor table, painting on the wall
Or shield of knight; only the rounded moon
Thro' the tall oriel on the rolling sea.
But always in the quiet house I heard,
Clear as a lark, high o'er me as a lark, 830
A sweet voice singing in the topmost tower
To the eastward: up I climb'd a thousand steps
With pain: as in a dream I seem'd to climb
For ever: at the last I reach'd a door,

A light was in the crannies, and I heard,
' Glory and joy and honour to our Lord
And to the Holy Vessel of the Grail.'
Then in my madness I essay'd the door ;
It gave ; and thro' a stormy glare, a heat
As from a seventimes-heated furnace, I,   840
Blasted and burnt, and blinded as I was,
With such a fierceness that I swoon'd away—
O, yet methought I saw the Holy Grail,
All pall'd in crimson samite, and around
Great angels, awful shapes, and wings and eyes.
And but for all my madness and my sin,
And then my swooning, I had sworn I saw
That which I saw ; but what I saw was veil'd
And cover'd ; and this Quest was not for me."

' So speaking, and here ceasing, Lancelot left   850
The hall long silent, till Sir Gawain—nay,
Brother, I need not tell thee foolish words,—
A reckless and irreverent knight was he,
Now bolden'd by the silence of his King,—
Well, I will tell thee : " O King, my liege," he said,
" Hath Gawain fail'd in any quest of thine ?
When have I stinted stroke in foughten field ?
But as for thine, my good friend Percivale,
Thy holy nun and thou have driven men mad,
Yea, made our mightiest madder than our least.   860
But by mine eyes and by mine ears I swear,
I will be deafer than the blue-eyed cat,
And thrice as blind as any noonday owl,
To holy virgins in their ecstasies,
Henceforward."

' " Deafer," said the blameless King,
" Gawain, and blinder unto holy things
Hope not to make thyself by idle vows,
Being too blind to have desire to see.
But if indeed there came a sign from heaven,
Blessed are Bors, Lancelot and Percivale, 870
For these have seen according to their sight.
For every fiery prophet in old times,
And all the sacred madness of the bard,
When God made music thro' them, could but speak
His music by the framework and the chord ;
And as ye saw it ye have spoken truth.

' " Nay—but thou errest, Lancelot : never yet
Could all of true and noble in knight and man
Twine round one sin, whatever it might be,
With such a closeness, but apart there grew, 880
Save that he were the swine thou spakest of,
Some root of knighthood and pure nobleness ;
Whereto see thou, that it may bear its flower.

' " And spake I not too truly, O my knights ?
Was I too dark a prophet when I said
To those who went upon the Holy Quest,
That most of them would follow wandering fires,
Lost in the quagmire ?—lost to me and gone,
And left me gazing at a barren board,
And a lean Order—scarce return'd a tithe— 890
And out of those to whom the vision came
My greatest hardly will believe he saw ;
Another hath beheld it afar off,
And leaving human wrongs to right themselves,

Cares but to pass into the silent life.
And one hath had the vision face to face,
And now his chair desires him here in vain,
However they may crown him otherwise.

' " And some among you held, that if the King
Had seen the sight he would have sworn the vow :　900
Not easily, seeing that the King must guard
That which he rules, and is but as the hind
To whom a space of land is given to plow.
Who may not wander from the allotted field
Before his work be done ; but, being done,
Let visions of the night or of the day
Come, as they will ; and many a time they come,
Until this earth he walks on seems not earth,
This light that strikes his eyeball is not light,
This air that smites his forehead is not air　910
But vision—yea, his very hand and foot—
In moments when he feels he cannot die,
And knows himself no vision to himself,
Nor the high God a vision, nor that One
Who rose again : ye have seen what ye have seen."

' So spake the King : I knew not all he meant.'

WILLIAM MORRIS

THE WRITING ON THE IMAGE

ARGUMENT

How on an Image that stood anciently in Rome were written certain words, which none understood, until a Scholar, coming there, knew their meaning, and thereby discovered great marvels, but withal died miserably.

    In half-forgotten days of old,
As by our fathers we were told,
Within the town of Rome there stood
An image cut of cornel wood,
And on the upraised hand of it
Men might behold these letters writ—
' PERCUTE HIC : ' which is to say,
In that tongue that we speak to-day,
' *Strike here!* ' nor yet did any know
The cause why this was written so.   10

    Thus in the middle of the square,
In the hot sun and summer air,
The snow-drift and the driving rain,
That image stood, with little pain,
For twice a hundred years and ten ;
While many a band of striving men
Were driven betwixt woe and mirth

Swiftly across the weary earth,
From nothing unto dark nothing:
And many an Emperor and King,
Passing with glory or with shame,
Left little record of his name,
And no remembrance of the face
Once watched with awe for gifts or grace.
   Fear little, then, I counsel you,
What any son of man can do;
Because a log of wood will last
While many a life of man goes past,
And all is over in short space.

   Now so it chanced that to this place
There came a man of Sicily,
Who when the image he did see,
Knew full well who, in days of yore,
Had set it there; for much strange lore,
In Egypt and in Babylon,
This man with painful toil had won;
And many secret things could do;
So verily full well he knew
That master of all sorcery
Who wrought the thing in days gone by,
And doubted not that some great spell
It guarded, but could nowise tell
What it might be. So, day by day,
Still would he loiter on the way,
And watch the image carefully,
Well mocked of many a passer-by.
   And on a day he stood and gazed
Upon the slender finger, raised

Against a doubtful cloudy sky,
Nigh noontide; and thought, 'Certainly
The master who made thee so fair
By wondrous art, had not stopped there,
But made thee speak, had he not thought
That thereby evil might be brought
Upon his spell.' But as he spoke,
From out a cloud the noon sun broke
With watery light, and shadows cold:
Then did the Scholar well behold
How, from that finger carved to tell
Those words, a short black shadow fell
Upon a certain spot of ground,
And thereon, looking all around
And seeing none heeding, went straightway
Whereas the finger's shadow lay,
And with his knife about the place
A little circle did he trace;
Then home he turned with throbbing head,
And forthright gat him to his bed,
And slept until the night was late
And few men stirred from gate to gate.
  So when at midnight he did wake,
Pickaxe and shovel did he take,
And, going to that now silent square,
He found the mark his knife made there,
And quietly with many a stroke
The pavement of the place he broke:
And so, the stones being set apart,
He 'gan to dig with beating heart,
And from the hole in haste he cast
The marl and gravel; till at last,

Full shoulder high, his arms were jarred,
For suddenly his spade struck hard
With clang against some metal thing :
And soon he found a brazen ring,
All green with rust, twisted, and great
As a man's wrist, set in a plate
Of copper, wrought all curiously
With words unknown though plain to see,
Spite of the rust : and flowering trees,
And beasts, and wicked images,   90
Whereat he shuddered : for he knew
What ill things he might come to do,
If he should still take part with these
And that Great Master strive to please.

    But small time had he then to stand
And think, so straight he set his hand
Unto the ring, but where he thought
That by main strength it must be brought
From out its place, lo ! easily
It came away, and let him see   100
A winding staircase wrought of stone,
Where through the new-come wind did moan.

    Then thought he, ' If I come alive
From out this place well shall I thrive,
For I may look here certainly
The treasures of a king to see,
A mightier man than men are now.
So in few days what man shall know
The needy Scholar, seeing me
Great in the place where great men be,   110
The richest man in all the land ?
Beside the best then shall I stand,

And some unheard-of palace have ;
And if my soul I may not save
In heaven, yet here in all men's eyes
Will I make some sweet paradise,
With marble cloisters, and with trees
And bubbling wells, and fantasies,
And things all men deem strange and rare,
And crowds of women kind and fair,   120
That I may see, if so I please,
Laid on the flowers, or mid the trees
With half-clad bodies wandering.
There, dwelling happier than the king,
What lovely days may yet be mine !
How shall I live with love and wine,
And music, till I come to die !
And then— Who knoweth certainly
What haps to us when we are dead ?
Truly I think by likelihead   130
Nought haps to us of good or bad ;
Therefore on earth will I be glad
A short space, free from hope or fear ;
And fearless will I enter here
And meet my fate, whatso it be.'

 Now on his back a bag had he,
To bear what treasure he might win,
And therewith now did he begin
To go adown the winding stair ;
And found the walls all painted fair   140
With images of many a thing,
Warrior and priest, and queen and king,
But nothing knew what they might be.

Which things full clearly could he see,
For lamps were hung up here and there
Of strange device, but wrought right fair,
And pleasant savour came from them.
  At last a curtain, on whose hem
Unknown words in red gold were writ,
He reached, and softly raising it
Stepped back, for now did he behold
A goodly hall hung round with gold,
And at the upper end could see
Sitting, a glorious company:
Therefore he trembled, thinking well
They were no men, but fiends of hell.
But while he waited, trembling sore,
And doubtful of his late-learned lore,
A cold blast of the outer air
Blew out the lamps upon the stair
And all was dark behind him; then
Did he fear less to face those men
Than, turning round, to leave them there
While he went groping up the stair.
Yea, since he heard no cry or call
Or any speech from them at all,
He doubted they were images
Set there some dying king to please
By that Great Master of the art;
Therefore at last with stouter heart
He raised the cloth and entered in
In hope that happy life to win,
And drawing nigher did behold
That these were bodies dead and cold
Attired in full royal guise,

And wrought by art in such a wise
That living they all seemed to be,
Whose very eyes he well could see,
That now beheld not foul or fair,
Shining as though alive they were.   180
And midmost of that company
An ancient king that man could see,
A mighty man, whose beard of grey
A foot over his gold gown lay;
And next beside him sat his queen
Who in a flowery gown of green
And golden mantle well was clad,
And on her neck a collar had
Too heavy for her dainty breast;
Her loins by such a belt were prest   190
That whoso in his treasury
Held that alone, a king might be.
On either side of these, a lord
Stood heedfully before the board,
And in their hands held bread and wine
For service; behind these did shine
The armour of the guards, and then
The well-attired serving-men,
The minstrels clad in raiment meet;
And over against the royal seat   200
Was hung a lamp, although no flame
Was burning there, but there was set
Within its open golden fret
A huge carbuncle, red and bright;
Wherefrom there shone forth such a light
That great hall was as clear by it
As though by wax it had been lit,

As some great church at Easter-tide.
  Now set a little way aside,
Six paces from the daïs stood
An image made of brass and wood,
In likeness of a full-armed knight
Who pointed 'gainst the ruddy light
A huge shaft ready in a bow.
  Pondering how he could come to know
What all these marvellous matters meant,
About the hall the Scholar went,
Trembling, though nothing moved as yet;
And for awhile did he forget
The longings that had brought him there
In wondering at these marvels fair;
And still for fear he doubted much
One jewel of their robes to touch.

  But as about the hall he passed
He grew more used to them at last,
And thought, ' Swiftly the time goes by,
And now no doubt the day draws nigh;
Folk will be stirring: by my head
A fool I am to fear the dead,
Who have seen living things enow,
Whose very names no man can know,
Whose shapes brave men might well affright
More than the lion in the night
Wandering for food:' therewith he drew
Unto those royal corpses two,
That on dead brows still wore the crown;
And midst the golden cups set down
The rugged wallet from his back,

Patched of strong leather, brown and black.
Then, opening wide its mouth, took up   240
From off the board, a golden cup
The King's dead hand was laid upon,
Whose unmoved eyes upon him shone
And recked no more of that last shame
Than if he were the beggar lame,
Who in old days was wont to wait
For a dog's meal beside the gate.
  Of which shame nought our man did reck,
But laid his hand upon the neck
Of the slim Queen, and thence undid   250
The jewelled collar, that straight slid
Down her smooth bosom to the board.
And when these matters he had stored
Safe in his sack, with both their crowns,
The jewelled parts of their rich gowns,
Their shoes and belts, brooches and rings,
And cleared the board of all rich things,
He staggered with them down the hall.
But as he went his eyes did fall
Upon a wonderful green stone,   260
Upon the hall-floor laid alone;
He said, ' Though thou art not so great
To add by much unto the weight
Of this my sack indeed, yet thou,
Certes, would make me rich enow,
That verily with thee I might
Wage one-half of the world to fight
The other half of it, and I
The lord of all the world might die;—
I will not leave thee;' therewithal   270

He knelt down midmost of the hall,
Thinking it would come easily
Into his hand ; but when that he
Gat hold of it, full fast it stack,
So fuming, down he laid his sack,
And with both hands pulled lustily,
But as he strained, he cast his eye
Unto the daïs, and saw there
The image who the great bow bare
Moving the bowstring to his ear ; 280
So, shrieking out aloud for fear,
Of that rich stone he loosed his hold
And catching up his bag of gold,
Gat to his feet : but ere he stood
The evil thing of brass and wood
Up to his ear the notches drew ;
And clanging, forth the arrow flew,
And midmost of the carbuncle
Clanging again, the forked barbs fell,
And all was dark as pitch straightway. 290
 So there until the judgment day
Shall come and find his bones laid low,
And raise them up for weal or woe,
This man must bide ; cast down he lay
While all his past life day by day
In one short moment he could see
Drawn out before him, while that he
In terror by that fatal stone
Was laid, and scarcely dared to moan.
But in a while his hope returned, 300
And then, though nothing he discerned,
He gat him up upon his feet,

And all about the walls he beat
To find some token of the door,
But never could he find it more,
For by some dreadful sorcery
All was sealed close as it might be,
And midst the marvels of that hall
This Scholar found the end of all.

But in the town on that same night, 310
An hour before the dawn of light,
Such storm upon the place there fell,
That not the oldest man could tell
Of such another : and thereby
The image was burnt utterly,
Being stricken from the clouds above ;
And folk deemed that same bolt did move
The pavement where that wretched one
Unto his foredoomed fate had gone,
Because the plate was set again 320
Into its place, and the great rain
Washed the earth down, and sorcery
Had hid the place where it did lie.
So soon the stones were set all straight,
But yet the folk, afraid of fate,
Where once the man of cornel wood
Through many a year of bad and good
Had kept his place, set up alone
Great Jove himself, cut in white stone,
But thickly overlaid with gold. 330
' Which,' saith my tale, ' you may behold
Unto this day, although indeed
Some Lord or other, being in need,

Took every ounce of gold away.'
But now, this tale in some past day
Being writ, I warrant all is gone,
Both gold and weather-beaten stone.

Be merry, masters, while ye may,
For men much quicker pass away.

MATTHEW ARNOLD

THE SICK KING IN BOKHARA

Hussein

O most just Vizier, send away
The cloth-merchants, and let them be,
Them and their dues, this day! the King
Is ill at ease, and calls for thee.

The Vizier

O merchants, tarry yet a day
Here in Bokhara! but at noon,
To-morrow, come, and ye shall pay
Each fortieth web of cloth to me,
As the law is, and go your way.

O Hussein, lead me to the King!   10
Thou teller of sweet tales, thine own,
Ferdousi's, and the others', lead!
How is it with my lord?

Hussein

                Alone,
Ever since prayer-time, he doth wait,
O Vizier! without lying down,
In the great window of the gate,

THE SICK KING IN BOKHARA

Looking into the Registàn,
Where through the sellers' booths the slaves
Are this way bringing the dead man.—
O Vizier, here is the King's door!

THE KING

O Vizier, I may bury him?

THE VIZIER

O King, thou know'st, I have been sick
These many days, and heard no thing
(For Allah shut my ears and mind),
Not even what thou dost, O King!
Wherefore, that I may counsel thee,
Let Hussein, if thou wilt, make haste
To speak in order what hath chanced.

THE KING

O Vizier, be it as thou say'st!

HUSSEIN

Three days since, at the time of prayer
A certain Moollah, with his robe
All rent, and dust upon his hair,
Watch'd my lord's coming forth, and push'd
The golden mace-bearers aside,
And fell at the King's feet, and cried:

'Justice, O King, and on myself!
On this great sinner, who did break
The law, and by the law must die!
Vengeance, O King!'

      But the King spake:
' What fool is this, that hurts our ears   40
With folly ? or what drunken slave ?
My guards, what, prick him with your spears !
Prick me the fellow from the path ! '
As the King said, so it was done,
And to the mosque my lord pass'd on.

But on the morrow, when the King
Went forth again, the holy book
Carried before him, as is right,
And through the square his way he took ;
My man comes running, fleck'd with blood   50
From yesterday, and falling down
Cries out most earnestly : ' O King,
My lord, O King, do right, I pray !

' How canst thou, ere thou hear, discern
If I speak folly ? but a king,
Whether a thing be great or small,
Like Allah, hears and judges all.

' Wherefore hear thou ! Thou know'st, how fierce
In these last days the sun hath burn'd ;
That the green water in the tanks   60
Is to a putrid puddle turn'd ;
And the canal, which from the stream
Of Samarcand is brought this way,
Wastes, and runs thinner every day.

' Now I at nightfall had gone forth
Alone, and in a darksome place
Under some mulberry-trees I found
 A little pool ; and in short space,

With all the water that was there
I fill'd my pitcher, and stole home
Unseen; and having drink to spare,
I hid the can behind the door,
And went up on the roof to sleep.

' But in the night, which was with wind
And burning dust, again I creep
Down, having fever, for a drink.

' Now meanwhile had my brethren found
The water-pitcher, where it stood
Behind the door upon the ground,
And call'd my mother; and they all,
As they were thirsty, and the night

Most sultry, drain'd the pitcher there;
That they sate with it, in my sight,
Their lips still wet, when I came down.

' Now mark! I, being fever'd, sick
(Most unblest also), at that sight
Brake forth, and cursed them—dost thou hear?—
One was my mother.—Now, do right!'

But my lord mused a space, and said:
' Send him away, Sirs, and make on!
It is some madman!' the King said.
As the King bade, so was it done.

The morrow, at the self-same hour,
In the King's path, behold, the man,
Not kneeling, sternly fix'd! he stood
Right opposite, and thus began,

Frowning grim down : ' Thou wicked King,
Most deaf where thou shouldst most give ear !
What, must I howl in the next world,
Because thou wilt not listen here ?

' What, wilt thou pray, and get thee grace,
And all grace shall to me be grudged ?
Nay but, I swear, from this thy path
I will not stir till I be judged ! '

Then they who stood about the King
Drew close together and conferr'd ;
Till that the King stood forth and said :
' Before the priests thou shalt be heard.'

But when the Ulemas were met,
And the thing heard, they doubted not ;
But sentenced him, as the law is,
To die by stoning on the spot.

Now the King charged us secretly :
' Stoned must he be, the law stands so.
Yet, if he seek to fly, give way ;
Hinder him not, but let him go.'

So saying, the King took a stone,
And cast it softly ;—but the man,
With a great joy upon his face,
Kneel'd down, and cried not, neither ran.

So they, whose lot it was, cast stones,
That they flew thick and bruised him sore.
But he praised Allah with loud voice,
 And remain'd kneeling as berore.

My lord had cover'd up his face;
But when one told him, ' He is dead,'
Turning him quickly to go in,
' Bring thou to me his corpse,' he said.

And truly, while I speak, O King,
I hear the bearers on the stair;   130
Wilt thou they straightway bring him in?
—Ho! enter ye who tarry there!

The Vizier

O King, in this I praise thee not!
Now must I call thy grief not wise.
Is he thy friend, or of thy blood,
To find such favour in thine eyes?

Nay, were he thine own mother's son,
Still, thou art King, and the law stands.
It were not meet the balance swerved,
The sword were broken in thy hands.   140

But being nothing, as he is,
Why for no cause make sad thy face?—
Lo, I am old! three kings, ere thee,
Have I seen reigning in this place.

But who, through all this length of time,
Could bear the burden of his years,
If he for strangers pain'd his heart
Not less than those who merit tears?

Fathers we *must* have, wife and child,
And grievous is the grief for these;   150
This pain alone, which *must* be borne,
Makes the head white, and bows the knees.

But other loads than this his own
One man is not well made to bear.
Besides, to each are his own friends,
To mourn with him, and show him care.

Look, this is but one single place,
Though it be great ; all the earth round,
If a man bear to have it so,
Things which might vex him shall be found. 160

Upon the Russian frontier, where
The watchers of two armies stand
Near one another, many a man,
Seeking a prey unto his hand,

Hath snatch'd a little fair-hair'd slave :
They snatch also, towards Mervè,
The Shiah dogs, who pasture sheep,
And up from thence to Orgunjè.

And these all, labouring for a lord,
Eat not the fruit of their own hands ; 170
Which is the heaviest of all plagues,
To that man's mind, who understands.

The kaffirs also (whom God curse !)
Vex one another, night and day ;
There are the lepers, and all sick ;
There are the poor, who faint alway.

All these have sorrow, and keep still,
Whilst other men make cheer, and sing.
Wilt thou have pity on all these ?
No nor on this dead dog, O King ! 180

THE SICK KING IN BOKHARA

The King

O Vizier, thou art old, I young!
Clear in these things I cannot see.
My head is burning, and a heat
Is in my skin which angers me.

But hear ye this, ye sons of men!
They that bear rule, and are obey'd,
Unto a rule more strong than their's
Are in their turn obedient made.

In vain therefore, with wistful eyes
Gazing up hither, the poor man,   190
Who loiters by the high-heap'd booths,
Below there, in the Registàn,

Says: 'Happy he, who lodges there!
With silken raiment, store of rice,
And for this drought, all kinds of fruits,
Grape-syrup, squares of colour'd ice,

'With cherries serv'd in drifts of snow.'
In vain hath a king power to build
Houses, arcades, enamell'd mosques;
And to make orchard-closes, fill'd   200

With curious fruit-trees brought from far
With cisterns for the winter-rain,
And, in the desert, spacious inns
In divers places—if that pain

Is not more lighten'd, which he feels
If his will be not satisfied;
And that it be not, from all time
The law is planted, to abide.

Thou wast a sinner, thou poor man!
Thou wast athirst; and didst not see, 210
That, though we take what we desire,
We must not snatch it eagerly.

And I have meat and drink at will,
And rooms of treasures, not a few.
But I am sick, nor heed I these;
And what I would, I cannot do.

Even the great honour which I have,
When I am dead, will soon grow still;
So have I neither joy, nor fame,
But what I can do, that I will. 220

I have a fretted brick-work tomb
Upon a hill on the right hand,
Hard by a close of apricots,
Upon the road of Samarcand;

Thither, O Vizier, will I bear
This man my pity could not save,
And, plucking up the marble flags,
There lay his body in my grave.

Bring water, nard, and linen rolls!
Wash off all blood, set smooth each limb! 230
Then say: ' He was not wholly vile,
Because a king shall bury him.'

ROBERT BROWNING

MULEYKEH

If a stranger passed the tent of Hóseyn, he cried ' A churl's!'
Or haply ' God help the man who has neither salt nor bread!'
—' Nay,' would a friend exclaim, ' he needs nor pity nor scorn
More than who spends small thought on the shore-sand, picking pearls,
—Holds but in light esteem the seed-sort, bears instead
On his breast a moon-like prize, some orb which of night makes morn.

What if no flocks and herds enrich the son of Sinán?
They went when his tribe was mulct, ten thousand camels the due,
Blood-value paid perforce for a murder done of old.
"God gave them, let them go! But never since time began,   10
Muléykeh, peerless mare, owned master the match of you,
And you are my prize, my Pearl: I laugh at men's land and gold!"

'So in the pride of his soul laughs Hóseyn—and right,
    I say.
Do the ten steeds run a race of glory? Outstripping
    all,
Ever Muléykeh stands first steed at the victor's staff.
Who started, the owner's hope, gets shamed and named,
    that day,
" Silence," or, last but one, is " The Cuffed," as we used
    to call
Whom the paddock's lord thrusts forth. Right, Hóseyn,
    I say, to laugh!'

'Boasts he Muléykeh the Pearl?' the stranger replies:
    ' Be sure
On him I waste nor scorn nor pity, but lavish both   20
On Duhl the son of Sheybán, who withers away in
    heart
For envy of Hóseyn's luck. Such sickness admits no
    cure.
A certain poet has sung, and sealed the same with an
    oath,
"For the vulgar—flocks and herds! The Pearl is a
    prize apart."'

Lo, Duhl the son of Sheybán comes riding to Hóseyn's
    tent,
And he casts his saddle down, and enters and ' Peace!'
    bids he.
' You are poor, I know the cause: my plenty shall mend
    the wrong.
'Tis said of your Pearl—the price of a hundred camels
    spent

MULÉYKEH

In her purchase were scarce ill paid : such prudence is
    far from me
Who proffer a thousand. Speak! Long parley may
    last too long.'   30

Said Hóseyn : ' You feed young beasts a many, of famous
    breed,
Slit-eared, unblemished, fat, true offspring of Múzennem :
There stumbles no weak-eyed she in the line as it climbs
    the hill.
But I love Muléykeh's face : her forefront whitens
    indeed
Like a yellowish wave's cream-crest. Your camels—go
    gaze on them!
Her fetlock is foam-splashed too. Myself am the richer
    still.'

A year goes by : lo, back to the tent again rides Duhl.
' You are open-hearted, ay—moist-handed, a very prince.
Why should I speak of sale ? Be the mare your simple
    gift!
My son is pined to death for her beauty : my wife prompts
    " Fool,   40
Beg for his sake the Pearl! Be God the rewarder, since
God pays debts seven for one : who squanders on Him
    shows thrift." '

Said Hóseyn : ' God gives each man one life, like a lamp,
    then gives
That lamp due measure of oil : lamp lighted—hold high,
    wave wide
Its comfort for others to share! once quench it, what
    help is left ?

The oil of your lamp is your son : I shine while Muléykeh
    lives.
Would I beg your son to cheer my dark if Muléykeh
    died ?
It is life against life : what good avails to the life-
    bereft ? '

Another year, and—hist ! What craft is it Duhl
    designs ?
He alights not at the door of the tent as he did last
    time,   50
But, creeping behind, he gropes his stealthy way by the
    trench
Half-round till he finds the flap in the folding, for night
    combines
With the robber—and such is he : Duhl, covetous up to
    crime,
Must wring from Hóseyn's grasp the Pearl, by whatever
    the wrench.

'He was hunger-bitten, I heard : I tempted with half
    my store,
And a gibe was all my thanks. Is he generous like
    Spring dew ?
Account the fault to me who chaffered with such an
    one !
He has killed, to feast chance comers, the creature he
    rode : nay, more—
For a couple of singing-girls his robe has he torn in
    two :
I will beg ! Yet I nowise gained by the tale of my wife
    and son,   60

'I swear by the Holy House, my head will I never wash
Till I filch his Pearl away. Fair dealing I tried, then
   guile,
And now I resort to force. He said we must live or
   die :
Let him die, then,—let me live! Be bold—but not too
   rash!
I have found me a peeping-place : breast, bury your
   breathing while
I explore for myself! Now, breathe! He deceived me
   not, the spy!

'As he said—there lies in peace Hóseyn—how happy!
   Beside
Stands tethered the Pearl : thrice winds her headstall
   about his wrist :
'Tis therefore he sleeps so sound—the moon through the
   roof reveals.
And, loose on his left, stands too that other, known far
   and wide,   70
Buhéyseh, her sister born : fleet is she yet ever missed
The winning tail's fire-flash a-stream past the thunderous
   heels.

'No less she stands saddled and bridled, this second, in
   case some thief
Should enter and seize and fly with the first, as I mean
   to do.
What then ? The Pearl is the Pearl : once mount her
   we both escape.'
Through the skirt-fold in glides Duhl,—so a serpent dis-
   turbs no leaf

In a bush as he parts the twigs entwining a nest : clean
    through,
He is noiselessly at his work : as he planned, he performs
    the rape.
He has set the tent-door wide, has buckled the girth, has
    clipped
The headstall away from the wrist he leaves thrice bound
    as before,   80
He springs on the Pearl, is launched on the desert like
    bolt from bow.
Up starts our plundered man : from his breast though
    the heart be ripped,
Yet his mind has the mastery : behold, in a minute more,
He is out and off and away on Buhéyseh, whose worth
    we know!

And Hóseyn—his blood turns flame, he has learned long
    since to ride,
And Buhéyseh does her part,—they gain—they are gain-
    ing fast
On the fugitive pair, and Duhl has Ed-Dárraj to cross
    and quit,
And to reach the ridge El-Sabán,—no safety till that be
    spied!
And Buhéyseh is, bound by bound, but a horse-length
    off at last,
For the Pearl has missed the tap of the heel, the touch of
    the bit.   90

She shortens her stride, she chafes at her rider the strange
    and queer :
Buhéyseh is mad with hope—beat sister she shall and must

Though Duhl, of the hand and heel so clumsy, she has to thank.
She is near now, nose by tail—they are neck by croup—joy! fear!
What folly makes Hóseyn shout ' Dog Duhl, Damned son of the Dust,
Touch the right ear and press with your foot my Pearl's left flank!'

And Duhl was wise at the word, and Muléykeh as prompt perceived
Who was urging redoubled pace, and to hear him was to obey,
And a leap indeed gave she, and evanished for evermore.
And Hóseyn looked one long last look as who, all bereaved, 100
Looks, fain to follow the dead so far as the living may :
Then he turned Buhéysch's neck slow homeward, weeping sore.

And, lo, in the sunrise, still sat Hóseyn upon the ground
Weeping : and neighbours came, the tribesmen of Bénu-Asád
In the vale of green Er-Rass, and they questioned him of his grief ;
And he told from first to last how, serpent-like, Duhl had wound
His way to the nest, and how Duhl rode like an ape, so bad !
And how Buhéyseh did wonders, yet Pearl remained with the thief.

And they jeered him, one and all: ' Poor Hóseyn is
    crazed past hope!
How else had he wrought himself his ruin, in fortune's
    spite?   110
To have simply held the tongue were a task for a boy or
    girl,
And here were Muléykeh again, the eyed like an antelope,
The child of his heart by day, the wife of his breast by
    night!'—
' And the beaten in speed!' wept Hóseyn: ' You never
    have loved my Pearl.'

                (By permission of Messrs. JOHN MURRAY.)

NOTES

I. MICHAEL

2. Ghyll is a short and for the most part a steep valley, with a stream running through it. W. W.

169. Clipping is the word used in the north of England for shearing. W. W.

258 ff. The story alluded to here is well known in the country. The chapel is called Ings Chapel. W. W.

III. LAMIA. PART I

46. Cirque-couchant means lying coiled in a circle.

58. Bacchus placed Ariadne's crown in heaven, where it forms the well-known constellation.

63. Proserpine was carried off from Sicily by Pluto, lord of Hades.

81. It was Hermes who led to Lethe, the river of forgetfulness, souls about to be re-embodied.

89. Hermes' magic wand wreathed with serpents was called the caduceus. Cp. line 133.

114. The psaltery was an ancient form of harp.

211, 212. 'Palatine' seems to be used as the adjective of 'palace,' and 'piazzian' suggests the pillared arcades of Italy (cp. line 361).

320. For the 'gardens of Adonis,' see Shakespeare, 1 *Henry VI.*, i. 6, 6.

333. Deucalion and Pyrrha, the Greek Noah and his wife, made new human beings by throwing stones over their shoulders.

375. Apollonius of Tyana was a famous philosopher, in whose *Life* the story of Lamia was first told.

PART II

160. Shakespeare uses the verb 'to daff,' meaning 'to thrust aside.'

183. Chapman often uses 'sphere' for 'circle.'

NARRATIVE POEMS

200. So Dryden had written of the 'well-vowelled' words of Italian.

226. Thyrsus was the Bacchic wand, wreathed with the vine.

236. A gnomed mine is a mine as the fancy may conceive it, peopled by sprites. The real thing is called a torched mine in *Isabella*.

260. So Macbeth says to Banquo's ghost : ' Thou hast no speculation in those eyes.'

'Philostratus, in his fourth book *De Vita Apollonii*, hath a memorable instance in this kind, which I may not omit, of one Menippus Lycius, a young man twenty-five years of age, that going betwixt Cenchreas and Corinth, met such a phantasm in the habit of a fair gentlewoman, which taking him by the hand, carried him home to her house, in the suburbs of Corinth, and told him she was a Phœnician by birth, and if he would tarry with her, he should hear her sing and play, and drink such wine as never any drank, and no man should molest him ; but she, being fair and lovely, would live and die with him, that was fair and lovely to behold. The young man, a philosopher, otherwise staid and discreet, able to moderate his passions, though not this of love, tarried with her a while to his great content, and at last married her, to whose wedding, amongst other guests, came Apollonius ; who, by some probable conjectures, found her out to be a serpent, a lamia ; and that all her furniture was, like Tantalus' gold, described by Homer, no substance but mere illusions. When she saw herself descried, she wept, and desired Apollonius to be silent, but he would not be moved, and thereupon she, plate, house, and all that was in it, vanished in an instant : many thousands took notice of this fact, for it was done in the midst of Greece.'

Burton's *Anatomy of Melancholy*, Part 3, Sect. 2, Memb. 1, Subs. 1.

IV. THE HOLY GRAIL

15. The pollen of the yew-tree in spring blows like smoke.

40. See line 697 for this guest.

49. The reference is to the Crucifixion. See *Matthew* xxvii. 50.

172. Tennyson meant the perilous seat of the old legend to stand for the spiritual imagination.

261. This line gives onomatopoeically the 'unremorseful flames.' A. T. Contrast line 715.

263. The golden dragon was Arthur's standard.

312. The White Horse was the emblem of the English or Saxons, as the dragon was of the Britons.
350. Wyvern = two-legged dragon.
421-440. Percivale finds fame as hollow as gold, wifely love, and the pleasures of sense.
453. The Magi are referred to.
661. The temples and upright stones of the Druidic religion. A. T. *E.g.* Stonehenge.
681. The Great Bear or Plough.
716. Talbots were heraldic dogs.
862. According to Darwin, white cats with blue eyes are generally deaf, if male.
907 ff. Tennyson here attempts to describe a recurring experience of his own. Cp. *The Ancient Sage*, ' And more, my son, for more than once when I . . .'

VI. THE SICK KING IN BOKHARA

12. Ferdousi (or Firdausi) was the Persian poet who tells the tale of *Sohrab and Rustum*.
31. Moolah (or mullah) is a Mohammedan learned in theology and sacred law.
63. Bokhara is a little distance from the river Zerafshan which flows by Samarcand.
109. Ulemas are Moslem judges; there is no priesthood in Islam.
167. Shiahs are an unorthodox sect of Moslems; Shiahism is the state religion of Persia.
173. ' Kaffirs ' is an Arabic word meaning ' infidels.'

VII. MULÉYKEH

16-18. The favourite is disgraced and nicknamed ' Silence '; or may even be last but one, and given the name of ' The Cuffed,' *i.e.* a horse cashiered by its owner.
42. Cp. Browning's poem, *The Patriot*, ' 'Tis God shall repay : I am safer so.'
61. The Holy House is the Bayt Ullah (House of Allah) or Caaba at Mecca, the Holy of Holies of Islam.
64. Cp. Spenser, *Fairy Queen*, iii. 11 *ad fin*.
114. Cp. Macduff's ' He has no children ' in *Macbeth*.

QUESTIONS AND SUBJECTS FOR ESSAYS

I. Michael

1. What is a pastoral mountain (5) ?
2. What is the use of the words ' of their own ' (8) ?
3. Explain ' natural ' (36), and ' telling ' (88).
4. What is meant by ' pottage ' (100) ? What does it usually mean ?
5. Explain ' card ' (106), and ' chimney ' (110).
6. How does Wordsworth pronounce ' utensil ' (115) ?
7. Have you met elsewhere the phrase ' a plot of rising ground ' (132) ?
8. What would we say in conversation for ' large prospect ' (133) ?
9. A child is sometimes called ' young hopeful.' Illustrate this from the poem.
10. Can you justify ' they ' in line 149 ?
11. How did the Boy's presence affect the Father's appreciation of nature ?
12. Pope wrote of ' paternal acres.' What is Wordsworth's equivalent, and what does the phrase mean ?
13. What was the choice mentioned in line 237 ?
14. What is a parish-boy (259) ?
15. Find one word to give the sense of line 347.
16. Expand ' hadst ' (352).
17. Explain ' burthened ' (374).
18. What is a covenant (414) ? Where have you met the word ?
19. What part of the story is very rapidly related ?
20. Can you suggest reasons for the following alterations of the original text ?—' pastime ' (155), dalliance ; ' threescore ' (373),

QUESTIONS AND SUBJECTS FOR ESSAYS 123

sixty; 'hale' (390), stout; 'to sun and cloud' (456), upon the sun.

21. Paraphrase lines 177-193.

---

1. Write a note on pastoral poems. What others of a different kind do you know?
2. Compare Pope's 'the proper study of mankind is man' with line 33, and indicate the contrasts in the work of the two poets. Would Pope have written line 32?
3. What do you know of Wordsworth's connexion with the English Lakes?
4. Mrs. Browning wrote of 'the scriptural grandeur of simplicity' in *Michael*. Illustrate this.
5. Consider the effect of this tale told in prose.

II. MAZEPPA'S RIDE

1. Consider the effect of interchanging 'horse' and 'steed' in the first two lines.
2. Parse 'day' (50).
3. What is the northern light (71)? Does it crackle?
4. What is a Spahi (80)? Cp. Sepoy.
5. How do autumnal eves nip foliage (116)?
6. Explain 'nerved' (154), cp. 246; and 'trunk' (180).
7. Explain line 163.
8. What is ignis-fatuus (262)? Have you ever heard of anybody seeing one?
9. What does 'had' stand for in line 264? Cp. 272.
10. Explain 'dapple into day' (289). What poet has written 'the dappled dawn'?
11. Write a note on 'booted it' (299).
12. What is a werst, or verst (307)?
13. What does 'reeking' mean (336)? Why is Edinburgh called 'Auld Reekie'?
14. Where are we given the word for 'that' in line 367?
15. Parse 'welcome' (378).
16. Who is the wretch in line 391?
17. Parse 'one day' (490). Is it ambiguous?
18. What is the more usual name of the Borysthenes?

NARRATIVE POEMS

19. What do you think of the conclusion ?
20. Paraphrase concisely lines 379-405. .

---

1. Read William of Deloraine's ride in *The Lay of the Last Minstrel*, and compare the two narratives.
2. Make a rough time-table of the ride.
3. Collect the similes, and notice how interest in his picture sometimes carries a poet beyond the points of resemblance.
4. Collect examples of alliteration, and say which you consider specially effective.
5. Can you account for the great diversity of the judgements passed on Byron's poetry by qualified critics ?
6. 'The Byronic in poetry is, in some respects, the contradictory of the Wordsworthian.' Illustrate this saying.

III. LAMIA. PART I.

1. What is the wreathed tomb of line 38 ? Why wreathed ? Cp. line 84.
2. Explain 'dove-footed' (42). What is Hermes doing ? Cp. line 66.
3. Write a note on 'gordian' (47).
4. What is a stooped falcon (67) ? a Phœbean dart (78) ? Circean head (115) ?
5. How does Keats pronounce 'weird' (107) ? 'syllabling' (244) ?
6. What is brede (158) ? the specious chaos (195) ?
7. What was Lycius thinking of in line 236 ?
8. Write a note on the use of 'far' (262); and on 'nice' (275).
9. What does line 288 refer to ?
10. What is the meaning of 'comprized' in line 347 ?
11. Comment on 'arch'd' (361).

PART II.

12. Explain line 55.
13. What is meant by 'dramatic irony' ? See lines 80, 81.
14. What does 'untasted' mean in line 132 ?
15. What was a sophist (172) ? What is the modern meaning of the word ?
16. What do you think of the mention of carpets in line 179 ?
17. What is meant by Ceres' horn (187) ?
18. What is osier'd gold (217) ?

19. What is meant by 'philosophy' in line 234, and how are rule and line its instruments?
20. Write a note on 'the many' (262).

---

1. Illustrate Keats's love of colour.
2. Discuss the sober truth of the famous passage II. 230-236.
3. What chief matters has Keats added to the original prose?
4. Pick out some of the most effective Alexandrines, or six-foot lines.
5. Describe the banquet hall in prose.

IV. THE HOLY GRAIL

1. What is the metaphor of lines 74, 75?
2. Find a word for the ideal of holiness conveyed in lines 98-100.
3. Comment on the metre of line 117. Contrast 692, 693.
4. Express line 151 in prose.
5. Do you see any connexion between the wings in lines 237 and 240?
6. Explain 'blazon' (248).
7. Why does Arthur refer to Taliessin and Lancelot in lines 300 ff.?
8. What are wandering fires (319)? What is Byron's word in *Mazeppa's Ride*?
9. Try to describe at length the appearance so vividly conveyed in lines 381, 382.
10. Where has the power of personality been already noted as in line 487?
11. What passage in the Bible does line 509 suggest?
12. What are 'they' in line 523?
13. Of what figure of speech is 'gossip and old wives' (553) an example?
14. Parse 'rejoice' (559): and 'I walking' (591).
15. Who is 'he' in line 667? Explain 'blows.'
16. What are the doors and house in lines 711, 712?
17. What are prophets compared to in lines 872 ff.?

---

1. Why did Arthur disapprove of the Quest? Contrast Gawain's attitude.
2. Point out the differences in the five visions of the Grail, and show how they correspond to differences of personality.

3. What do you understand by losing oneself to find oneself ? How was it done in the five cases ?
4. Give some examples of Tennyson's great powers of observation.
5. 'No one has more exalted the sense of hearing than Tennyson.' Illustrate this.
6. Collect some lines (a) with a strong pause after the first syllable ; (b) with trisyllabic feet ; (c) of smooth sound ; (d) of harsh sound. Try to find some significance in each case.

V. The Writing on the Image

1. Parse ' full shoulder high ' (81).
2. What is the reference in line 94 ?
3. Parse ' laid ' (122).
4. Write a note on ' likelihead ' (130).
5. Parse ' nothing ' (143), and ' curtain ' (148).
6. Can you account for the pleasant savour from the lamps (147)?
7. What happy life (172) ?
8. What is the subject of ' held ' in line 195 ?
9. Explain ' open golden fret ' (203). Is there anything like it in *Lamia* ?
10. What proverb is suggested by line 225 ?
11. What would you say for ' wage ' in line 267 ?
12. Write a note on ' notches ' (286). What is the usual form of the word ?
13. Can you illustrate the tendency to associate storms with human events, in history and in fiction ?

---

1. Contrast the life and work of Morris with those of his master, Chaucer.
2. Do you know any other tales of underground adventures ?
3. Write a panegyric on fairy tales.
4. What other poets besides Morris were considerable writers of prose ?
5. What other poems do you know written in these octosyllabic couplets ? How did Scott and Byron vary the metre ? What is noticeable in Morris's treatment of it ?

VI. The Sick King in Bokhara

1. How much per cent. were these dues (3) ? See line 8.
2. Account for line 20.

QUESTIONS AND SUBJECTS FOR ESSAYS 127

3. What is the Registàn (17) ?
4. Explain ' golden mace-bearers ' (34).
5. What other poets have delighted in the sound of 'Samarcand' ?
6. Write a note on ' stole ' (70).
7. What is the advantage, from the social point of view, of stoning as a method of capital punishment ?
8. What figure of speech occurs in line 133 ? Cp. 1 *Corinthians*, xi. 17.
9. Explain the reference to balance and sword in lines 139, 140.
10. Explain ' fretted ' (221).

---

1. What difference of form do you notice between this and the other narratives here printed ? What are the advantages and the drawbacks of the form ?
2. Why was the King so sad ?
3. It has been said that the only thing worth having in this world is one's own way. Is it true ? How does this tale bear on the saying ?
4. Contrast the style of this poem with that of *Lamia*.

VII. MULÉYKEH.

1. What is the man doing in line 4 ?
2. Explain fully the transaction referred to in lines 8, 9.
3. What should we say for ' victor's staff ' (15) ?
4. What is actually happening in lines 1-24 ?
5. Paraphrase lines 28-30.
6. What is the point of ' weak-eyed ' (33) ?
7. What is the meaning of ' dry-fisted ' ?
8. What does Hóseyn claim in lines 43-48 ?
9. What is the trench for (51) ?
10. State in prose the sequence of Duhl's thoughts in lines 55-60.
11. What did Buhéyseh ever miss (72) ?
12. What did Muléykeh perceive in line 97 ?
13. Contrast the run of lines 84 and 102.

---

1. What is the explanation of Hóseyn's shout ? Could Byron have written a poem like this ?
2. Write a note on the use of outlandish proper names in poetry, considering the practice of Milton and Scott.

3. Read Mr. Kipling's *Ballad of East and West* and compare the two narratives.

4. How does the dramatic method affect the probability of some of Duhl's remarks?

5. Which of the poems in this book do you prefer? Give your reasons.

6. What other narrative poets do you know? What about Macaulay? Make a list of poems which you would include if you were making a selection.

HELPS TO FURTHER STUDY

1. Matthew Arnold's *Selections from Wordsworth* in the Golden Treasury Series (Macmillan) should be read and pondered on. Myers's *Life* (English Men of Letters) and Sir W. Raleigh's *Wordsworth* are both fine.

2. Byron's longer poems are very unequal. Read *The Siege of Corinth*, and the wonderful satire *The Vision of Judgement*. Moore's *Life* is long, but very interesting.

3. The best essay on Keats is that by Dr. Bridges, Poet Laureate (Muses Library), and W. T. Arnold is most interesting on his language (Globe Library). Sir Sidney Colvin's *Life* is the best and fullest, and Mr. E. de Sélincourt's edition of the poems (Methuen) has valuable notes.

4. The *Memoir* of Tennyson by his son is full of interest. The *Works* with notes by the author (Macmillan) should be constantly in the hands of every lover of poetry. A good recent study is Mr. Harold Nicolson's *Tennyson* (Constable, 1923).

5. Read *The Life and Death of Jason,* and as much as you can of *The Earthly Paradise*. The *Life* by Mr. J. W. Mackail is good; also shorter studies of his life and work by Clutton-Brock (Home University Library) and Holbrook Jackson (Cape, 1926).

6. *Sohrab and Rustum* is perhaps Arnold's only popular poem, but he is eminently companionable to thoughtful readers. Swinburne greatly admired *The Sick King*. Arnold's *Essays in Criticism* and *Lectures on Translating Homer* are simply full of good things. Mr. Birrell's essay in *Res Judicatae* is delightful.

ENGLISH LITERATURE SERIES

General Editor: J. H. FOWLER, M.A.
LATE ASSISTANT MASTER AT CLIFTON COLLEGE.

1. **ADDISON—ESSAYS FROM.** Edited by J. H. FOWLER, M.A. Limp, 1s. 6d. Boards, 1s. 9d.
2. **ANDERSEN—STORIES FROM.** Selected by Mrs. P. A. BARNETT. Limp, 1s. 3d. Boards, 1s. 6d.
3. **ARABIAN NIGHTS—STORIES FROM.** Edited by A. T. MARTIN, M.A. Limp, 1s. 3d. Boards, 1s. 6d.
108. **ARNOLD—PROSE SELECTIONS FROM MATTHEW ARNOLD.** Edited by Prof. E. T. CAMPAGNAC.
4. **AUSTEN—PRIDE AND PREJUDICE.** Abridged by H. A. TREBLE, M.A. 1s. 6d.
5. **— SENSE AND SENSIBILITY.** Abridged and Edited by Mrs. F. S. BOAS. Illustrated. 2s.
6, 7. **BALLADS OLD AND NEW.** Selected and Edited by H. B. COTTERILL, M.A Part I., 1s. 9d. Part II., Limp, 1s. 3d. Boards, 1s. 6d.
8. **BATES—A NATURALIST ON THE AMAZONS.** Abridged and Edited by F. A BRUTON, M.A. 80 Illustrations. 2s. 6d.
9. **BORROW—WANDERINGS IN SPAIN.** Edited by F. A. CAVENAGH, M.A Limp, 1s. 6d. Boards, 1s. 9d.
10, 11. **BRITAIN—TALES OF OLD.** By E. P. ROBERTS. Part I. Limp, 1s. 3d. Boards, 1s. 6d. Part II. Limp, 1s. 3d. Boards, 1s. 6d.
12. **BROWNING—SELECTIONS FROM.** Edited by Mrs M. G. GLAZEBROOK. 1s. 6d.
110. **— PIPPA PASSES.** Edited by Dr. E. A. PARKER.
120. **— BALAUSTION'S ADVENTURE.** By Dr. E. A. PARKER.
13, 14. **BUCKLEY—CHILDREN OF THE DAWN. Old Tales of Greece.** By E. F. BUCKLEY. With Introduction by A. SIDGWICK, Notes and Subjects for Essays by J. H. FOWLER. Part I, 1s 6d. Part II., Limp, 1s 3d Boards, 1s 6d.
15. **BUNYAN—PILGRIM'S PROGRESS.** Abridged and Edited by C. F. KNOX, M.A. 1s 9d.
16. **BYRON—CHILDE HAROLD.** Cantos III. and IV. Edited by J. H. FOWLER, M.A. Limp, 1s. 6d. Boards, 1s. 9d.
17. **CARLYLE—ABBOT SAMSON.** Chapters from "Past and Present," Book II. Edited by F. A. CAVENAGH, M.A. Limp, 1s. 6d. Boards, 1s 9d
18, 19. **— HEROES AND HERO-WORSHIP.** Edited by H. M. BULLER, M.A. 2 vols. Vol. I., 2s. Vol. II., 2s.
20. **CAVENDISH—LIFE OF WOLSEY.** Edited by MARY TOUT, M.A. Limp, 1s 3d. Boards, 1s. 6d
21. **CERVANTES—DON QUIXOTE.** Abridged and Edited by C. F. KNOX. Limp, 1s. 9d. Boards, 2s.
22. **COBBETT—RURAL RIDES—Selections.** Edited by GUY BOAS. 1s. 9d.
23. **DEFOE—ROBINSON CRUSOE.** Abridged and Edited by J. HUTCHISON. 2s.
24. **DICKENS—DAVID COPPERFIELD.** Abridged by H. A. TREBLE, M.A. Limp, 1s 6d Boards, 1s. 9d
25. **— A CHRISTMAS CAROL.** Edited by C. F. KNOX. Limp, 1s. 3d. Boards, 1s 6d
26. **— A TALE OF TWO CITIES.** Abridged and Edited by C. H RUSSELL, M.A. 1s. 9d.
27. **— NICHOLAS NICKLEBY.** Abridged and Edited by C. F. KNOX. 1s 9d.
109. **— THE OLD CURIOSITY SHOP.** Abridged and Edited by D. M. STUART. 1s. 9d.

ENGLISH LITERATURE SERIES.—*Continued.*

28. DUMAS—THE THREE MUSKETEERS. Abridged and Edited by C. J. BROWN, M.A., and H. S. WALKER, M.A. 1s. 9d.

29. ELIOT—SILAS MARNER. Abridged by MAY COSSEY. Limp, 1s. 6d. Boards, 1s. 9d.

113 FROUDE—HISTORY OF ENGLAND. Chapter I. Edited by E. H. BLAKENEY.

30. GASKELL—CRANFORD. Abridged and Edited by Mrs. F. S. BOAS. Illustrated. Limp, 1s. 6d. Boards, 1s 9d.

31. GIBBON—THE AGE OF THE ANTONINES. (Chapters I.-III. of the Decline and Fall.) Edited by J. H. FOWLER, M.A. Limp, 1s. 3d. Boards, 1s 6d.

32. — THE DECLINE AND FALL OF THE ROMAN EMPIRE, Narratives from. Selected and Edited by J. H. FOWLER, M.A. First Series. Limp, 1s. 3d. Boards, 1s. 6d.

33. GOLDSMITH—VICAR OF WAKEFIELD. Abridged by Mrs. F. S. BOAS. 1s. 9d.

116. — THE GOOD-NATURED MAN. Edited by ROBERT HERRING.

117. — SHE STOOPS TO CONQUER. Edited by ROBERT HERRING.

34. GRIMM—FAIRY TALES—A Selection. Edited by A. T. MARTIN, M.A. Limp, 1s. 3d. Boards, 1s. 6d.

35. HAWTHORNE—STORIES FROM A WONDER-BOOK FOR GIRLS AND BOYS. Edited by J. H. FOWLER, M.A. Limp, 1s. 6d. Boards, 1s 9d.

36, 37. — TANGLEWOOD TALES. Edited by J. H. FOWLER, M.A. Part I., Limp, 1s. 3d. Boards, 1s. 6d. Part II., Limp, 1s. 6d. Boards, 1s. 9d.

38. HINDU TALES FROM THE SANSKRIT. Translated by S. M. MITRA. Edited by Mrs. A. BELL. Limp, 1s. 6d. Boards, 1s. 9d.

39, 40, 41, 42. HISTORY—A BOOK OF POETRY ILLUSTRATIVE OF ENGLISH. Edited by G. DOWSE, B.A. Part I. A.D. 61-1485. Part II. The Tudors and Stuarts. Part III. The Hanoverian Dynasty. 1s. each. The 3 parts in 1 vol., 2s 6d.

43. INDIAN HISTORY—TALES FROM. By Mrs. A. S. ROE. Limp, 1s. 3d. Boards, 1s. 6d.

44. IRVING—RIP VAN WINKLE, The Legend of Sleepy Hollow, and other Sketches. Edited by H. M. BULLER, M.A. Limp, 1s. 6d. Boards, 1s. 9d.

45. KEARY—HEROES OF ASGARD. By A. and E. KEARY. Adapted and Edited by M. R. EARLE. 1s. 9d.

46. KEATS—Selections. Edited by B. GROOM, M.A. 1s. 6d.

47. KINGSLEY—ANDROMEDA, with the Story of Perseus prefixed. Edited by GEORGE YELD, M.A. Limp, 1s. 3d. Boards, 1s. 6d

48, 49. LAMB—TALES FROM SHAKESPEARE. Edited by H. A. TREBLE, M.A. First Series. Limp, 1s. 3d. Boards, 1s. 6d. Second Series. Limp, 1s. 6d. Boards, 1s. 9d.

50. LONGER NARRATIVE POEMS (18th Century). Edited by G. G. LOANE, M.A. Limp, 1s. 3d. Boards, 1s. 6d.

51. LONGER NARRATIVE POEMS (19th Century). First Series. Edited by G. G. LOANE, M.A. 1s. 6d.

114. LONGER NARRATIVE POEMS (19th Century). Second Series. Edited by G. G. LOANE, M.A.

52. LONGFELLOW—SHORTER POEMS. Edited by H. B. COTTERILL, M.A. Limp, 1s. 3d. Boards, 1s. 6d.

53. MACAULAY—ESSAY ON SIR W. TEMPLE. Edited by G. A. TWENTYMAN, M.A. Limp, 1s. 6d. Boards, 1s. 9d.

54. — ESSAY ON FRANCES BURNEY. Edited by A. D. GREENWOOD. Limp, 1s. 3d. Boards, 1s. 6d.

55. — ESSAY ON CLIVE. Edited by H. M. BULLER, M.A. Limp, 1s. 6d. Boards, 1s. 9d.

ENGLISH LITERATURE SERIES.—Continued.

56. **MACAULAY—ESSAY ON WARREN HASTINGS.** Edited by H. M. BULLER, M.A. Limp, 1s. 9d. Boards, 2s.
57. **— NARRATIVES FROM.** Edited by F. JOHNSON. Limp, 1s. 6d. Boards, 1s. 9d.
58. **— ESSAY ON ADDISON.** Edited by R. F. WINCH, M.A. Limp, 1s. 6d. Boards, 1s. 9d.
59. **MALORY—MORTE D'ARTHUR.** Selections Edited by DOROTHY M. MACARDLE. Limp, 1s. 3d. Boards, 1s. 6d.
60. **MODERN POETRY—A FIRST BOOK OF.** Selected and Arranged by H A. TREBLE, M.A. 1s. 6d.
61. **MODERN POETRY—A SECOND BOOK OF.** Selected and Arranged by H. A. TREBLE, M.A. 1s. 6d.
115. **MODERN POETRY—A THIRD BOOK OF.** Selected and Arranged by H. A. TREBLE, M.A.
63. **MODERN LYRICS—GOLDEN TREASURY OF.** Edited by L. BINYON. With Notes by J. H. FOWLER, M.A. Book I., 2s. 3d. Book II., 2s. 3d.
64. **MORRIS—LIFE AND DEATH OF JASON.** Abridged and Edited by R. W. JEPSON, B.A. Limp, 1s. 6d. Boards, 1s 9d.
65. **MOTLEY—THE RISE OF THE DUTCH REPUBLIC.** Narratives from. Selected and Edited by J. HUTCHISON. Limp, 1s. 6d. Boards, 1s. 9d.
66. **NAPIER—HISTORY OF THE PENINSULAR WAR** Narratives from. Edited by M. FANSHAWE, B.A. Limp, 1s. 3d Boards, 1s 6d
67. **NJAL AND GUNNAR.** Edited by H. MALIM, M.A. Limp, 1s. 6d. Boards, 1s 9d.
68. **ODYSSEY—THE BOY'S.** By W. C. PERRY. Edited by T. S. PEPPIN, M.A. Limp, 2s. 3d. Boards, 2s. 6d.
69. **ORATORS—BRITISH.** Passages Selected and Arranged by J. H. FOWLER, M.A. Limp, 1s. 3d. Boards, 1s 6d.
70. **PANDAV PRINCES, THE.** Edited by WALLACE GANDY. 1s 9d.
71. **PARKMAN—PIONEERS OF FRANCE IN THE NEW WORLD.** Selections from. Edited by KENNETH FORBES, M.A. Limp, 1s. 3d. Boards, 1s. 6d
118. **PATER.—SELECTIONS.** Edited by Mrs. P. A. BARNETT.
72. **PEACOCK—MAID MARIAN.** Edited by F. A. CAVENAGH, M.A. Limp, 1s. 6d. Boards, 1s 9d.
73. **PERSIAN HERO, A. Stories from the "Shah Nameh."** Edited by W. GANDY. Limp, 1s 6d Boards, 1s 9d.
74. **PLUTARCH—LIFE OF ALEXANDER.** North's Translation. Edited by H. W. M. PARR, M.A. Limp, 1s. 3d. Boards, 1s. 6d.
75. **— LIFE OF JULIUS CAESAR.** North's Translation. Edited by H. W. M. PARR, M.A. Limp, 1s 6d Boards, 1s. 9d.
76. **PROSE—FIRST BOOK OF ENGLISH FOR REPETITION.** Passages Chosen and Arranged by J. H. FOWLER, M.A. Limp, 1s. 3d. Boards, 1s 6d
77. **PROSE—FOR REPETITION.** Selected and Arranged by NORMAN L. FRAZER, M.A. Limp, 1s. 3d. Boards, 1s 6d.
78. **PROSE—SEVENTEENTH CENTURY.** Selected and Edited by E. LEE. Limp, 1s. 3d. Boards, 1s. 6d.
79. **RAMA, PRINCE OF INDIA, WANDERINGS OF.** Edited by W. GANDY. Limp 1s. 3d. Boards, 1s 6d.
80. **REYNARD THE FOX.** Edited by H. A. TREBLE, M.A. Limp, 1s. 3d. Boards, 1s. 6d.
81. **RUSKIN—CROWN OF WILD OLIVE.** Edited by J. H. FOWLER, M.A. Limp, 1s. 3d. Boards, 1s. 6d.
82. **— SESAME AND LILIES.** Edited by A. E. ROBERTS, M.A. Limp, 1s. 3d. Boards, 1s. 6d.

ENGLISH LITERATURE SERIES.—*Continued.*

83. **RUSKIN—SELECTIONS FROM "THE STONES OF VENICE."** Edited by Dr. E. A. PARKER. 1s. 9d.
84. **SCOTT—IVANHOE.** Abridged and Edited by F. JOHNSON. Limp, 2s. 3d. Boards, 2s. 6d.
85. **— THE TALISMAN.** Abridged and Edited by F. JOHNSON. Limp, 2s. 3d. Boards, 2s. 6d.
86, 87. **— TALES OF A GRANDFATHER.** Abridged and Edited by J. HUTCHISON. First Series. Limp, 1s. 3d. Boards, 1s. 6d. Second Series. Limp, 1s. 3d. Boards, 1s. 6d.
88, 89. **SERTUM: A GARLAND OF PROSE NARRATIVES.** Selected and Edited by J. H. FOWLER and H. W. M. PARR. Book I. Sixteenth to Eighteenth Centuries. Limp, 1s. 3d. Boards, 1s 6d. Book II. Nineteenth Century. Limp, 1s. 3d. Boards, 1s. 6d.
90. **SHAKESPEARE—Select Scenes and Passages from the English Historical Plays.** Edited by C. H. SPENCE, M.A. Limp, 1s. 3d. Boards, 1s 6d.
91. **— MIDSUMMER-NIGHT'S DREAM.** Edited by P. T. CRESWELL, M.A. Limp, 1s. 3d. Boards, 1s. 6d.
92. **SHELLEY—Selections.** Edited by E. H. BLAKENEY, M.A. 1s. 6d.
112. **SHERIDAN—SCHOOL FOR SCANDAL.** Edited by R. HERRING.
119. **— THE RIVALS.** Edited by ROBERT HERRING.
93. **SIDNEY—DEFENCE OF POESY.** Edited by D. M. MACARDLE. Limp, 1s. 3d. Boards, 1s. 6d.
94. **SOUTHEY—EPISODES FROM LIFE OF NELSON.** Edited by C. H. SPENCE, M.A. Limp, 1s. 3d. Boards, 1s 6d.
95. **SPENSER—TALES FROM.** By SOPHIA H. MACLEHOSE. Limp, 1s. 9d. Boards, 2s
96. **STEVENSON—TRAVELS WITH A DONKEY.** Edited by R. E. C. HOUGHTON, M.A. 1s. 9d.
97. **— VIRGINIBUS PUERISQUE AND OTHER PAPERS.** Edited by J. H. FOWLER, M.A. 1s. 9d.
98. **— AN INLAND VOYAGE.** Edited by R. E. C. HOUGHTON, M.A. 1s. 9d.
99. **STOW—A SURVEY OF LONDON.** Selections from, Edited by A. BARTER. Limp, 1s. 3d. Boards, 1s. 6d.
100. **SWIFT—GULLIVER'S TRAVELS.** Abridged and Edited by G. C. EARLE, B.A. 1s. 9d.
101. **THACKERAY—THE ROSE AND THE RING.** Edited by D. M. STUART. 1s. 9d.
111. **— ESMOND.** Abridged and Edited by D. M. STUART.
102. **THOREAU—CHAPTERS FROM WALDEN.** Edited by A. CRUSE. Limp, 1s. 6d. Boards, 1s. 9d.
103. **TROY—THE TALE OF.** Re-told in English by Aubrey Stewart. Edited by T. S. PEPPIN, M.A. Limp, 2s. 3d. Boards, 2s. 6d.
104. **WHITE—SELBORNE—Selections.** Edited by F. A. BRUTON, M.A. 40 Illustrations. Limp, 1s. 6d. Boards, 1s 9d.
105. **WORDSWORTH—PRELUDE. Selections, including Book V.** Edited by B. GROOM, M.A. 1s. 6d.
106, 107. **YONGE—A BOOK OF GOLDEN DEEDS.** By CHARLOTTE M. YONGE. Abridged and Edited by Mrs. H. H. WATSON. Parts I. and II. Limp, 1s. 6d. Boards, 1s. 9d. each.

MACMILLAN AND CO., LTD., LONDON